CLASSIC
STYLE

CLASSIC
STYLE

JUDITH MILLER

PHOTOGRAPHY BY TIM CLINCH

SIMON &
SCHUSTER
EDITIONS

SIMON & SCHUSTER EDITIONS
Rockefeller Center
1230 Avenue of the Americas
New York, NY 10020

Special Photography **Tim Clinch**

Chief Contributor **John Wainwright**

Contributor **Claire Weatherall**

Executive Editor **Judith More**

Executive Art Editor **Janis Utton**

Project Editor **Arlene Sobel**

American Editors **Roslyn Siegel (Senior Editor)**

Andrea Au (Assistant Editor)

Layout Design **Tony Spalding**

Production Controller **Paul Hammond**

First published in Great Britain in 1998 by
Mitchell Beazley, an imprint of Reed Consumer
Books Limited
Michelin House, 81 Fulham Road
London SW3 6RB
also in Auckland

Library of Congress Cataloging-in-Publication Data
Miller, Judith.
Classic style / Judith Miller : photography by Tim
Clinch.
p.   cm.
Simultaneously published in Great Britain by
Mitchell Beazley.
Includes index.

1. Decoration and ornament–Classical influences.
I. Clinch, Tim. II. Title.
NK1710.M56   1998
745.4'441–dc21
                                                    98-18915
                                                    CIP

ISBN 0-684-84997-6
Manufactured in China
10 9 8 7 6 5 4 3 2 1

CONTENTS

FOREWORD

Having traveled extensively throughout Europe and America over the last twelve years, researching and photographing houses and apartments for numerous books and television programmes on interior design and architecture, my most lasting impression is of the enduring presence of Classical-style architecture, decoration, and ornament. I can think of very few cities and major towns that don't display in most, or at least much, of their domestic and civic architecture the Classical principles of construction and styles of ornamentation that were originated in Ancient Greece and Rome between the 7th century B.C. and approximately 300 A.D. Equally, the vast majority of both domestic and civic interiors boast, at the very least, architectural fixtures and fittings inspired by Classical prototypes, while a very large number are entirely decorated and furnished in a Classical style.

Part of the explanation for this lies in the esthetically appealing symmetry and proportion inherent in Classical Greco-Roman architecture, decoration, furnishings, and artifacts—at a very fundamental level, they just somehow seem "right." At the same time, much of Classicism's popularity also resides in the sheer richness, elegance, and diversity of its decorative motifs and imagery—a vocabulary of ornament which, since the 14th century and the beginning of the Renaissance, has been continually embellished and reinterpreted in order to accommodate the changing preoccupations of different generations. Indeed, it is the resulting diversity of Classical styles through the centuries—from Renaissance, through 17th-century Baroque, early 18th-century Palladian Revival, mid-18th-century Rococo, and late 18th- and early 19th-century Neoclassicism, to 20th-century Modernism and contemporary Postmodernism—that is especially appealing today. Not only do all of these major styles, and their national and regional variations, offer architects, interior designers, and professional and amateur decorators alike, a vast range of inspirational material, they also provide a fundamental link with the cradle of our civilization—a reassuring continuity that will undoubtedly ensure the future of Classic style.

THE HISTORY OF CLASSIC STYLE

Appreciation of Classicism in architecture and design since the Renaissance recognizes that "Greek (and Roman) architecture, while the fruit of all the civilizations which preceded the great period of Greek (and Roman) culture, did not live for itself alone; for it has sown the seed of European (and American) architecture, and has determined the Future form and growth of most subsequent European art."

(William Bell Dinsmore, 1950)

ANCIENT GREECE & ROME

Classical Greek and Roman (Greco-Roman) architecture gradually evolved from the 7th century B.C. until the decline of the Roman Empire in the 4th century A.D. Devised by the Ancient Greeks and greatly elaborated by the Romans, it was to provide a vocabulary of ornament that has been almost constantly revived and reinterpreted from the 14th- to 16th-century Renaissance to the present day.

The primary system of Greco-Roman ornament, and the basis of Classical architecture, were the Orders: Doric, Ionic, and Corinthian (used by both the Greeks and Romans); Composite (a mixture of the Ionic and Corinthian developed by the Romans); and Tuscan (Roman, but derived from the ancient civilization of Etruria centered in Tuscany, in Italy, from the 7th to the 2nd centuries B.C.). Each order consisted of a column, usually mounted on a base (in some cases a pedestal or a plinth), topped by a capital (a plain or ornamented block) and supporting an entablature (a horizontal beam divided into a cornice, frieze, and architrave). The entablature ran across the top of, and therefore linked, a series of columns. Apart from the relative proportions of the basic components of each Order, the primary differences between them were determined by the degree of ornamentation of the capital and entablature. The Doric, for example, was relatively plain and considered rather "masculine"; the Ionic

Above Classical architecture in the 18th and 19th centuries was popularized by illustrations of archaeological finds, such as this Roman ruin, published by Henry Abbot in England in 1820.

more "feminine"; the Corinthian heavily ornamented; the Composite a compromise between the Ionic and the Corinthian; and the Tuscan stubby, unornamented and "rustic."

As to the style of ornamentation of the Orders, this ranged from simple rectilinear moldings (*see* pages 52–55) to motifs and imagery largely based on plant forms, figures, and scenes from Greco-Roman mythology, and artifacts symbolic of war, religion, and domesticity. Notable among the numerous plant forms were acanthus leaves, anthemia, palmettes, grapevines, and laurel leaves–these were often used to form festoons, rosettes, and scrolling foliage, and were sometimes used with representations of human figures and animals.

The majority of the motifs and imagery carved into the capitals and entablatures of the Orders were also employed in Greco-Roman (especially Roman) interior decoration, notably in wall-paintings–known as "grotesques" in Ancient Rome. Augmented with images of urns, vases, birds, and mythical creatures such as sphinxes (human head; body of a lion) and griffins (head, wings, and claws of an eagle; body of a lion), they were also often applied to furniture (*see* pages 72–79) and other artifacts (*see* pages 82–91). When combined with the principles of architectural construction inherent in the Orders, they provided a rich and varied source of forms and motifs for the many subsequent Classical revivals.

Above These elaborate trompe l'oeil wall decorations in a Roman villa at Boseoreale, near Pompeii, Italy, date to the 1st century A.D. Incorporating theatrical masks and faux marble columns, they are derived from a Greek stage set of ca. 30–40 A.D.

Below The Greek Ionic Order was developed by the Ionian people of the Aegean islands and the coast of Asia Minor. This early example–the temple of Artemis at Ephesus–is by Cretan architect Chersiphron of Knossos, and dates to ca. 560–550 A.D.

Right The impressive display of Classical architectural fixtures and fittings in Peter Hone's apartment in London, England, includes original Greek and Roman pieces, and many late 18th-, early 19th-, and 20th-century Coade stone and plaster copies.

Above Herculaneum, a Roman city near Naples, Italy, was discovered in 1709 and excavated at intervals from 1738–1820. It proved a rich source of secular Roman architecture and ornament for late 18th- and early 19th-century Neoclassicists, such as Robert Adam and Karl Schinkel.

RENAISSANCE TO BAROQUE

Having largely fallen out of favor following the fall of the western Roman Empire in the 5th century A.D., Classical Greco-Roman architecture and ornament (*see* pages 10–11) was reborn during the course of the 14th, 15th, and 16th centuries–a period known as the Renaissance. The revival, which began in Italy, and was primarily inspired by archaeological excavations of the architecture and artifacts that had survived from Ancient Rome, resulted in the reintroduction of Roman or Roman-inspired Orders (also *see* pages 10–11), and Classical architectural devices, such as temple-front porticoes, pediments, round-headed arches, and rusticated (large stone-block) masonry. Classical Roman motifs, such as acanthus leaves, scrolling foliage, swags and festoons, *pateras* and scallop shells, were also readopted, and these were applied not only as architectural ornament (often with *grisaille*–monochromatic trompe l'oeil wall decorations), but also to furniture, textiles, and decorative artifacts such as vases and urns.

By the 16th century, Renaissance architecture and ornament had begun to diverge into two related but increasingly distinct styles. The "High Renaissance" Classicism of architects such as Andrea Palladio (*see* pages 14–15) strove to preserve the integrity and purity of original Roman forms, and provided the inspiration for early 18th-century Classical architecture throughout Europe and the United States (*see* pages 16–17). Conversely, the

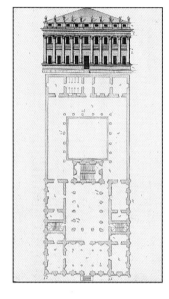

Above Italian architect Andrea Palladio (1508–80) played a fundamental role in the dissemination of the theories and forms of Classical architecture, mainly via treatises illustrated with engravings, such as the example above.

"Mannerism" of architects such as Michelangelo and Giulios Romano elaborated upon Classical Roman forms, such as columns and brackets, in a highly sculptural way, and often employed them purely for visual effect, without reference to their original structural purpose.

Mannerism's highly ornamental interpretation of Classical architecture proved increasingly popular during the latter part of the 16th century, and gave rise to the flamboyant Baroque style that became fashionable throughout most of Europe, notably Italy, Germany, Austria, France (under the patronage of Louis XIV), and England.

There were, of course, regional variations. For example, German and Austrian Baroque was lighter and more exuberant than the heavier and more grandiose French version. However, all variations were characterized by elaborate effects, in which ornament based on human figures, angels, and cupids spilled over onto Classical pediments, cornices, and arches, while other architectural elements, notably roof lines, gables, and broken pediments, were embellished with vast scrolls and volutes (spiral, scrolling forms), urns, and flaming torches. In interiors, considerable use was also made of mirrors and extravagant painted trompe l'oeil decoration which, when combined with the highly sculptural forms and opulent ornamentation of Baroque furniture (with carvings, marbles, and semiprecious stones), merely added to the theatricality of the style.

Left The Banqueting House, built 1619–22, in London, is recognized as English architect Inigo Jones's masterpiece. Its "solid, proporsionable ... masculine and unaffected" interiors are strongly influenced by the works and writings of the Italian architect, Andrea Palladio.

Right A heavily Classical version of Baroque decoration and architecture flourished in France under the patronage of Louis XIV, who reigned from 1638–1715. The *Galerie des Glaces* (Hall of Mirrors), conceived by Charles Le Brun and Jules Hardouin-Mansart for the Palace of Versailles, epitomizes the grandeur of the style.

Right The elaborate, sculptural forms characteristic of 17th-century Baroque architecture and ornament are evident in this ornate plaster ceiling and fireplace at Castle Twichel, in the Netherlands. The fireplace, typical of Dutch Baroque, features voluptuously carved scrollwork on the wooden fire-surround and overmantel, an ornate marble relief sculpture (dated to 1550) framed within the overmantel, and delft tiles lining the sides of the hearth.

Right The Villa Barbaro, designed by Andrea Palladio and built 1550–60 in Naser, Italy, is a *tour de force* of Renaissance architecture and decoration. The elaborate *trompe l'oeil* wall decorations are by Paulo Veronese.

ELEMENTS OF

PALLADIAN STYLE

The Italian architect Andrea Palladio (1508–80) had a profound influence on the development of Western architecture from the mid-16th century onward, notably in the work of English architect Inigo Jones in the 17th century, and in the Palladian Revival of the early 18th century (*see* pages 16–17). Palladio's theories of architecture and design were disseminated via the illustrations he provided for the 1556 reissue of the Roman Vitruvius's account of Classical architecture, *De Architettura,* and in his own *I Quattro Libri dell'Architettura* (published in 1570), which covered the Classical Orders, domestic and public buildings, and temples. Similarly influential were the numerous churches, palaces, and villas he designed in Italy. The hallway and salon shown left are in the Villa Barbaro, which was built ca. 1550–60 in Maser, near Venice, for the brothers Daniele and Marcantonio Barbaro. These interiors display the elegance, serenity, harmony, and proportion characteristic of Palladio's work. Equally magnificent are the extensive trompe l'oeil frescoes. These are the work of Venetian painter Paolo Veronese, and are masterfully blended into Palladio's architecture.

1. Engaged columns and pilasters (pillars) are a recurring feature of Palladio's interiors. However, the fluted column in the foreground is actually part of Veronese's architecturally sympathetic trompe l'oeil frescoes, and is derived from the Roman Corinthian Order. It features a capital of acanthus leaves, *caulicoli* (stalks), and volutes (scrolls). In the room beyond, rectangular, fluted, trompe l'oeil pilasters flank the mantelpiece.

2. This elegant, Classical-style door frame has a triangular pediment (low-pitched gable). Embellishments are restricted to egg-and-dart (oval-and-V-shapes) and bead moldings; the tympanum (triangular-shaped center section of the pediment) and frieze (the upper part of the wall) are left characteristically plain.

3. Also part of the trompe l'oeil wall decorations, this Roman arch is faced with lyre-shaped motifs. These are interspersed with *pateras* (oval or round dishes decorated with a formalized flower or rosette), and are filled with various fruits (mostly grapes). In the Classical vocabulary of ornament, grapes are generally used to symbolize Bacchus (the Roman god of wine and fertility).

4. *Aegricanes* (goats' heads) and *cornucopias* (stylized goats' horns overflowing with ears of wheat and fruit) were popular Classical Greek and Roman ornament, and were revived during the Renaissance. The *aegricane* (above the arch) originally symbolized ritual sacrifice. The *cornucopias* (flanking the head above the pediment) symbolized fertility and abundance, or peace and concord, and are attributes of Bacchus and also of Ceres (the Roman goddess of agriculture).

5. Large mantelpieces, with Classical architectural moldings or carvings on their jambs, consoles, lintels, friezes, and overmantels, became the focal point of most grand reception rooms during the Renaissance.

6. Trompe l'oeil murals feature in many of Palladio's interiors. They were employed in Classical Greek and Roman buildings as a means of enhancing the sense of light, enlarging the proportions of a room, and providing a "view" of the world outside. Favored subjects included gardens, temples, ruins, harbors, seashores, rivers, and fountains, as well as deities and mythological figures set in landscapes. Here, Veronese has also included one of the Barbaros' dogs.

7. This wrought-iron chair, with brass finials on the back and arms, is inspired by the Greek *thronos* (throne-chair) and Greco-Roman X-frame stools.

8. The stone flooring throughout the Villa Barbaro is typical of grander 16th-century interiors. The contrast between the uniformly patterned stone floor (foreground) and geometrically patterned tiles (in the salon beyond) helps to emphasize the division of rooms.

THE AGE OF ELEGANCE

Two very distinct styles of architecture, ornament, and decoration dominated the first half of the 18th century: Palladianism and Rococo. Palladianism was a Classical revival that emerged in England at the beginning of the century as a reaction to the grandiose excesses of ornamentation of 17th-century Baroque style (*see* pages 12–13), which the influential Scottish architect Colen Campbell described as a "affected and licentious." Promoted chiefly by Campbell and Lord Burlington, an amateur architect and patron of the arts, Palladianism was primarily based on the

Above **The Gallery, like the other interiors at Chiswick House, in London, England, displays the perfection of proportion and detail inherent in the Palladianism of architect William Kent and his patron, Lord Burlington.**

buildings and published observations of the 16th-century Italian architect Andrea Palladio (*see* pages 14–15), as well as on the work of the 17th-century English architect Inigo Jones (*see* pages 12–13). Classical Roman–not Greek–in origin, the style in its purest form was characterized by bold, austere, and, in the grandest houses, massive architectural elements, such as temple-front porticoes, Giant Orders (*see* pages 12–13), rusticated masonry (large blocks of stone separated by deep joints), tripartite, arch-topped Venetian windows, and vaulted (coffered) ceilings. Ultimately, however, the style, which was widely adopted in Russia, Prussia, and the United States (see pages 22–23) towards the middle of the 18th century, relied for effect–in houses both large and small–not upon sheer scale, but on harmony of proportion and detail.

Rococo style emerged in France following the death of Louis XIV in 1715, and was a reaction to the excessively formal and overly heavy Baroque style that had flourished under his patronage since the late 1630s. Early Rococo style (also called *Régence* style because it developed from 1715–23, when the Duc d'Orléans was Regent to the infant Louis XV) was characterized by a delicacy of ornament which made much use of diaper patterns (repeated geometric patterns employed as a framework for motifs such as formalized flowers or leaves), light scrollwork, and scallop-shell motifs. In these respects it retained much of the Classical symmetry of earlier Baroque ornamentation. During the 1720s, however, Rococo style became more extravagant and markedly asymmetrical. Primarily used for interior decoration, this later phase of the Rococo was typified by a softening of the angles of geometric patterns into curves or curls, and by the adoption of exotic Chinese, Turkish, and Indian imagery–notably *singerie* (monkey) motifs; all were combined with naturalistic sprigs of foliage or flowers and with the more abstract forms of rocaille (rock and shellwork–from which Rococo derived its name). Although Rococo endured in France until Louis XV's death in 1774, and was widely adopted in Europe, notably southern Germany, it made little impact in America, or in England, where its frivolity met with disapproval.

Left The Duke de la Gardi's study at the Tullgarn Palace, built in 1719 near Stockholm, shows the influence of contemporary French decoration in Sweden–namely, the lighter, more elegant Classicism that followed the Baroque and heralded the Rococo.

Right The abundance of timber in America in the 18th century resulted in a greater use of wall-paneling in comparison to Europe. However, as in this Connecticut interior, the Classical division of the wall into frieze, field, and dado was usually retained in the configuration of the paneling.

Above This bedroom in a 20th-century New York apartment has been reconstructed and decorated in 18th-century Rococo style. The predominantly cream and pale gray-green color scheme, and the curving forms of the fireplace, tables, chairs, and canopied *lit à la polonaise* (Polish-style bed), are typically Rococo.

Left Chiswick House, in London, England, was built by the 3rd Earl of Burlington in the late 1720s. The Blue Velvet Room shown here was its centerpiece and epitomize early Palladian decoration, particularly in its sumptuous blue color scheme enlivened with richly gilded architectural moldings and furniture.

NEOCLASSICISM
IN EUROPE

The Neoclassical movement emerged in Europe around the middle of the 18th century, and endured in various guises throughout Europe, as well as America (*see* pages 24–25), until the mid-19th century. Initially a reaction to the excesses of Rococo-style ornament and decoration (*see* pages 16–17), Neoclassicism was inspired by what the Society of Dilettanti (founded in London, England, in 1732) described as "Grecian taste and Roman spirit," and was fueled by the archaeological excavations of Classical Greek and Roman cities and towns, notably Herculaneum (beginning in 1738) and Pompeii (starting in 1755), in southern Italy. The architectural forms and decorative motifs and imagery, especially the fresco wall decorations, unearthed at these sites during the second half of the 18th and early 19th centuries, provided a wealth of new information on the Greco-Roman vocabulary of ornament. Moreover, this inspirational reference material was widely disseminated throughout Europe and America by architects, interior designers, craftsmen, and patrons of the arts alike, who either personally visited the sites on the Grand Tour (*see* page 82–91), or gained access to them via the writings and the pattern books of architects and archaeologists such as the Italian, Giovanni Battista Piranesi.

Above **The engravings of Giovanni Piranesi (1720–78), widely disseminated throughout Europe, helped to fuel the development of Neoclassicism. This is his section of the Pantheon, in Rome, Italy.**

Piranesi's promotion of the richness and diversity of not only Greek and Roman architecture and ornament, but also Etruscan and Ancient Egyptian precedents–via publications such as *Il Campo Marzio dell'antica Roma* (1762), *Diverse Maniere d'Adornare i Cammini* (1769), and *An Apologetical Essay in Defence of the Egyptian and Tuscan Architecture* (also 1769)–was enthusiastically taken up by Robert Adam in England, and thus played a major role in the development of Neoclassical Adam style (*see* pages 22–23). Similarly, Piranesi's engravings (together with Robert Adam's designs) also provided much of the inspiration for the emergence of Neoclassicism (the "*goût antique*" or old style) in France during the reign of Louis XVI (*see* Normandy Château, pages 140–45).

Following the execution of Louis XVI in 1795, and under the rule of the Directoire (1795–99), French Neoclassical decoration and ornament became less elaborate, and drew more heavily on severer Greek Forms (*see* Paris Apartment, pages 158–63). However, under the patronage of Napoleon Bonaparte and his Empress Josephine, French Empire style supplanted the Directoire style and, via the work of designers Charles Percier and Pierre Fontaine, reintroduced Imperial Roman motifs and combined

Left Haga Palace was built 1787–90 for Gustav III of Sweden. This interior illustrates the restrained Neoclassical style of decoration that supplanted the more flamboyant Rococo in Sweden in the late 18th century.

Right The frieze of a typical Adam fireplace, in the Tapestry Room at Osterley Park House, in Middlesex, England, incorporates a series of scagliola (imitation marble) plaques devised to copy Florentine Renaissance hardstone mosaics.

Right Neoclassical Adam ceilings were segmented and embellished with plaster moldings, painted decoration, or both. This centerpiece at Newby Hall, in Yorkshire, England, features a central roundel painted with figures from Classical mythology.

Above The synthesis of Greek and Roman motifs and imagery characteristic of many Robert Adam interiors is clearly evident in the plaster moldings in the entrance hall of Osterley Park House. Notable elements include acanthus leaves, scrolling foliage, trophies-of-arms, swags, festoons, and Greek keys.

them with Etruscan, Ancient Egyptian, and military motifs–the latter to reflect Napoleon's military conquests (*see* American Empire Style, pages 26–27).

During the first two decades of the 19th century, French Empire style became the height of fashion in many European countries, notably Sweden, where French emigrées had played a major role in determining the national taste in architecture and decoration since the early 18th century. Indeed, the transition in Sweden from mid-18th-century Swedish Rococo, through late 18th-century Swedish Gustavian style–a variant of Neoclassical Louis XVI style (also *see* Normandy Château, pages 140–45)–to early 19th-century Swedish Empire style not only specifically reflects the considerable influence of the French in the development of European (and American) Neoclassicism, but also generally highlights the extensive cross-fertilization of styles of architecture and ornament between countries during this period.

In England, for example, early 19th-century Regency style (*see* pages 28–29) was initially inspired by the opulent Neoclassicism of Louis XVI, and went on to accommodate numerous elements of French Empire style. However, due to the emnity between the England and France during the Napoleonic wars, many aspects of Empire style were omitted from Regency interiors, notably some of the Imperial Roman motifs favored by Napoleon, as well as his personal emblems, such as the bee and the swan. Indeed, in drawing more heavily on Greek ornament and decoration than the predominantly Roman-based Empire style, the English Regency illustrates the highly varied and eclectic nature of Neoclassicism during the early 19th century, when Classical Greek and Roman motifs and imagery were either combined or, as in the Greek Revival in Germany (*see* pages 32–33), employed exclusively.

Left Decorated in 1794, the library at Elghammar Manor in Sweden is an example of the Swedish-Palladian style popular in Scandinavia during the late 18th century.

Below French Empire style proved even more fashionable than Neo-Palladianism in early 19th-century Sweden. This bedroom, with its gilded stucco walls and striped fabrics, epitomizes the style.

Left Although built ca. 1765, during the French vogue for curvaceous Rococo ornament, the Château de Morsan, in Normandy, features more austere, rectilinear embellishments that herald late 18th-century Neoclassicism.

Below Neoclassical motifs, patterns, and imagery dominate this early 19th-century Empire-style entrance hall in Sweden. Also note the architectural prints pasted to the walls.

ELEMENTS OF

ADAM STYLE

The Little Drawing Room, shown left, at Audley End, a large Jacobean house in Essex, England, was remodeled in 1764 by Robert Adam (1728–92). Together with his less influential brothers James and John, Robert established the distinctive Adam (or Neoclassical) style of architecture, decoration, and ornament during the second half of the 18th century. First fashionable in Britain, it also made an impact, chiefly via pattern books, in France, Italy, Germany, and Russia, as well as in America, where it formed the basis of early Federal style. Inspiration for Adam style was highly eclectic, and lay in the buildings of Roman antiquity and the Italian Renaissance, and in a large repertoire of decorative elements derived from the Ancient Greek and the Etruscan vocabularies of ornament. Lighter and more elegant than the earlier Palladian and later Greek Revival styles (*see* pages 32–33), Adam style was widely admired for the grandeur of its architectural effect, the subtlety evident in its deployment of distinctive motifs, and, above all, the manner in which it sympathetically and successfully integrated the architecture of a building with the design of its interiors.

1. The ceiling is decorated with *guilloche,* a repeating ornament of interlacing circular bands, the centers of which are embellished with rosettes and other stylized floral and leaf forms. The *guilloche,* which was frequently used in Greco-Roman Classical ornament and often features in Adam interiors, is used in linear form as a small band around the base of the frieze.

2. The ornamentation of the frieze is typical of Adam style. The military trophies were originally employed by the Greeks and Romans as celebrations of victory. The festoons, hung from ribbons and made up of strings of husks, are derived from the fruit and floral garlands hung in Greek and Roman temples. The figurative panels are inspired by Etruscan decorations.

3. Robert Adam made extensive use of grotesques as wall decorations, and commissioned the painter Rebecca Biagio to produce these examples. Grotesques were based on Classical Roman wall paintings discovered in Rome in 1488. The Roman originals mainly consisted of animals, birds, and mythological animals set within foliate (decorated with carved leaves) scrolls. Most of these basic elements were retained during the Renaissance, but were placed in vertical panels and "hung" in a more structured, candelabralike form. In the 18th century, the discovery of more grotesques from antiquity helped fuel their popularity in Neoclassical interiors.

4. Six-paneled doors became almost standard during the 18th century. The most prestigious examples were constructed from polished hardwoods, notably mahogany, and the most exotic were inlaid with finely figured woods such as ebony, holly, or cherry. However, many were of deal (fir or pine) and either woodgrained to simulate expensive hardwoods or, as here, painted with images derived from Pompeiian and Etruscan vocabularies of ornament.

5. The Adam brothers designed many elaborate architectural door surrounds based on the Classical Orders. This reeded pilaster has acanthus leaves on its capital, and is one of a pair which, with a pair of fluted columns, supports an entablature (architrave, frieze, and cornice) decorated with Neoclassical motifs.

6. Like all the furniture the Adam brothers designed, the carving, painting, gilding, and upholstery on the Roman-inspired stools and double-stool is specifically designed to complements the Neoclassical decorations and ornament employed throughout the room.

7. Boards of polished oak or, as here, unvarnished fir or pine were the most common types of flooring in the 18th century. However, fitted carpet, either English with geometrical patterns, or of Eastern origin with floral designs, was sometimes installed in the principal reception rooms of the grandest houses.

NEOCLASSICISM IN AMERICA

Neoclassical architecture and decoration in America broadly reflected its European counterparts (*see* pages 18–21), and can be roughly divided into two overlapping styles: Federal style and Greek Revival. Federal style emerged just prior to the Declaration of Independence in 1776 and endured throughout the early decades of the 19th century. In its earliest stages, Federal style was largely based on Neoclassical Adam style (*see* pages 22–23), with exteriors characterized by delicate columns, arch-top windows, and fanlights, and interiors more richly decorated with Classical motifs such as festoons, *pateras*, rosettes, urns, and scrolling foliage. However, early Federal style also accommodated a purer, sterner, Roman form of Neoclassicism, which initially ran parallel with the Adam style, but by the end of the 18th century had largely superseded it. Promoted by Thomas Jefferson, the third President of the United States, as an appropriate architectural language for the new republic, it was partly inspired by early 18th-century English Palladian designs (*see* pages 16–17), partly by French Neoclassicism under the reign of Louis XVI and during the Directoire (*see* pages 18–21), and partly by original Roman buildings, notably the Roman temple Maison Carré that had survived at Nîmes in southern France.

Above Neoclassical elements in this hallway of a New York apartment include a geometric-pattern tiled floor, Greco-Roman urns, a side-table with acanthus leaf and lion's paw carvings, and a picture of Roman ruins.

During the early part of the 19th century, French Neoclassical taste continued to exert considerable influence on architects and designers, especially in relation to interior decoration and ornament. This became particularly evident during the second two decades of the century, when French Empire style was enthusiastically adopted and as American Empire style became the height of fashion (*see* pages 26–27). However, while Empire style drew heavily on the Classical Roman vocabulary of ornament, the exteriors of many new American buildings began to reflect the revival of Classical Greek architecture. Fueling this development were architects such as Benjamin Latrobe, who as early as 1798 had incorporated the rather severe Classical Greek Ionic Order (*see* pages 10–11) in the Bank of Pennsylvania, in Philadelphia. During the 1830s and 1840s, the interiors of many American houses also adopted the Greek Revival style of decoration and ornament (*see* pages 32–33) that had superseded Empire style in much of Europe. However, by this stage American Neoclassical architecture and decoration had developed beyond being a mere copy of European models–the integration of native motifs (corncobs, tobacco leaves, stars, and, especially, the bald eagle) having given it a distinctive American flavor.

Right Saturated red color scheme, enlivened with gilding, were fashionable in early 19th-century reception rooms, as in the Music Room of Richard Jenrette's American Empire-style house on the Hudson River, in New York State. The American rosewood-and-gilt, damask-upholstered furniture dates to 1823.

Below Third President of the United States, Thomas Jefferson remodeled his house, Monticello, ca. 1796–1808. The dining room is a blend of Palladian architecture and Neoclassical decorations and furnishings.

Below Mount Vernon, in Virginia, was built and furnished ca. 1760–87 by George Washington, the first President of the United States. The view across the entrance hall to the Little Parlor shows the influence of Classical architecture and ornament during this period. Prominent features include the door frames—the plainer with a broken pediment, the grander with fluted pilasters and egg-and-dart and dentil moldings. The latter, painted in fashionable Prussian blue, a color also used on the wall-paneling, provides a cool, elegant contrast to the polished hardwood woodwork.

ELEMENTS OF
AMERICAN EMPIRE STYLE

The room shown left is in the Morris Jumel Mansion, in Harlem, New York. It was originally decorated and furnished in Empire style during the 1820s, after the owner's wife returned from a trip to Paris where she bought a large collection of furnishings and accessories that were then the height of fashion in France and much of Europe. Like many of the other rooms in the mansion, this bedroom displays most of the key decorative elements that constitute the Empire style established in the late 1790s and early 1800s by leading French architects and designers, Charles Percier and Pierre

Fontaine. Particularly notable are the walls, plain-papered in a brilliant green (bright yellow and crimson were also fashionable), and divided into frieze, field, and dado by monochromatic, trompe l'oeil paper cutouts featuring Classical motifs. Also typical of the style is the coordination of the soft furnishings in terms of both fabric and color. Thus, the green of the carpet echoes that of the walls. Similarly, the reverse of the swagged-and-tailed silk drapes above the *lit-en-bateau* (boat-shaped bed) is picked up in the electric blue bedcover, bolster, and upholstered curricle (side-chair).

1. "King of the Birds," the eagle has been a symbol of power and victory since Assyrian times. It was borne on the standards of the Roman legions, and was the emblem of the Holy Roman Empire. After Napoleon adopted the eagle as a military emblem in 1804, it rapidly became one of the key motifs of Empire style. The indigenous bald eagle, classically postured with spread wings, was also chosen as a national emblem by the Americans, as an assertion of patriotism and independence following the Revolutionary War.

2. This elaborate, swagged wallpaper frieze features Classical motifs, such as vases, lyres, ribbons, and foliage, typical of Empire style. Together with the paper dado rail and paper infill above the baseboard (both also displaying Classical motifs), it separates the wall into the Classical division of frieze, field, and dado. The paper is a documentary reproduction of the original paper brought over from France in 1826 by the mansion's owners.

3. A bed placed "military style" with its side against the wall, underneath swagged-and-tailed drapes hung from a wall-mounted corona and brass rosettes, is typical of many French and American Empire-style interiors. The silk drapes are edged with "campaign" (bell-shaped tassel) fringing, an example of decorative trimming that remained popular throughout the 19th century.

4. This fine example of a French Empire-style *lit-en-bateau* (boat-shaped bed) features decorative brass mounts. It was given to the Jumels in 1826 by Princess Hortense of France, and was supposedly used by Napoleon when he was First Consul of the French Republic.

5. Brass stars were popular motifs on Neoclassical Empire and Regency furniture and were often used as ornamental bolt-heads to lock wooden joints. The palm motif, emblematic of Roman personifications of Fame and Victory, also appears on Neoclassical furniture.

6. The fitted, hand-knotted woven pile carpet was a feature of many grander Empire-style interiors. The majority of designs incorporated Classical (as here) or Egyptian motifs, and often echoed the configuration of the plasterwork on the ceiling. Prior to the 1790s, the leading makers were the workshops at Savonnerie and Aubusson in France, and at Axminster and Wilton in England. Thereafter, centers of production were also established in Philadelphia, Pennsylvania.

7. This French-made Empire-style curricle (side-chair) is constructed from mahogany and features saber legs and a silk-upholstered back and seat.

8. Emanating from France, Empire-style decoration was largely inspired by the political and military exploits of Napoleon Bonaparte–the subject of this portrait–and flourished under the patronage of his consort, Josephine de Beauharnais.

THE ENGLISH REGENCY

The English Regency was the period from 1811 to 1820 when George, Prince of Wales, ruled England as the Prince Regent due to the sickness of his father, George III. However, what was to become known as Regency style emerged via the patronage of Prince George as early as the late 1780s, and remained popular until the end of his reign as George IV in 1830.

Regency style was initially inspired by the Prince of Wales's passion for the Neoclassical architecture and decoration that was fashionable in France during the reign of Louis XVI (1774–92). The refinement and grandeur of French taste that characterized early Regency style was encapsulated in the interiors of the Prince's London residence, Carlton House, and at Southill Park, in Bedfordshire. Devised by the architect Henry Holland, and executed mainly by French craftsmen, they featured classically correct, predominantly rectilinear architectural embellishments–columns, pilasters, friezes, and architraves–that provided the perfect foil for the precise arrangements of mirror glass, crystal chandeliers, and fine French furniture.

Around the turn of the 19th century, Regency style began to change as French Empire style (*see* pages 18–21) emerged under the patronage of Napoleon Bonaparte and swept first across Europe and later America (*see* pages 26–27). However, although English architects and designers drew heavily on French Empire style, they

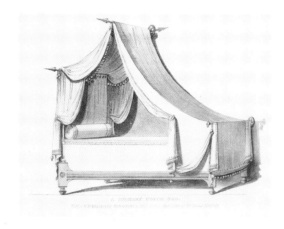

Above This French-style military couch bed appeared in Ackermann's *Repository of Arts.* First issued in England in 1811, this book disseminated fashionable furnishing schemes among the increasingly affluent middle classes of Regency England.

did not simply copy it. For example, while French interiors were dominated by replications and adaptations of the architectural ornament of Ancient Rome, Regency interiors combined Roman motifs and imagery with Classical Greek equivalents (*see* pages 32–33) and elements of *Le Style Etrusque* (*see* pages 18–21). Moreover, because of the Napoleonic wars and the enmity between England and France, Napoleonic motifs, such as the bee and the swan (respectively, Napoleon's and his consort Josephine's personal emblems), were not adopted by the English.

Further differences between English Regency and French Empire style lay in the former's incorporation of architectural elements, such as pointed arches, window tracery, and battlements, all derived from the Medieval Gothic vocabulary of ornament. Also, while exotic chinoiserie-based schemes were absent from French interiors, they did appear in grander Regency houses in England–most notably the Brighton Pavilion, in Brighton, Sussex–although they were generally confined to one or two rooms. However, common to French Empire and English Regency styles were Ancient Egyptian motifs and imagery, such as palm trees and sphinxes, whose popularity was fueled by the French and English military campaigns in North Africa and, in England, by Admiral Nelson's victory over Napoleon's navy at the Battle of the Nile in 1798.

Below With its exotic Egyptian palm tree columns, lavish swagged drapes, and gilded "Dolphin Suite" furniture, the South Drawing Room at the Brighton Pavilion, in Brighton, England, is the quintessential Regency fantasy.

Right Plas Teg, a Jacobean house in North Wales, displays the symmetrical furnishing arrangements of Regency interiors. Also characteristic are the striped wallpaper, classically inspired vases, console table, and X-frame stool.

Left The sense of warmth, light, and space in the South Drawing Room at Sir John Soane's House–built from 1792 to 1824, in London, England–is enhanced by bright, sulphur-yellow walls, drapes, and upholstered furniture, and by cut-glass chandeliers, and large, strategically placed mirrors.

Above right Egyptian, as well as Classical Greek and Roman ornament, was employed in Regency interiors. This Egyptianesque head–one of a pair–adorns the arm of an English Regency chair in Bill Blass's New York apartment.

BATTLE OF THE STYLES

During the first half of the 19th century the styles of architecture and decoration most fashionable on both sides of the Atlantic were essentially Neoclassical. These included French Empire (*see* pages 18–21), American Empire (*see* pages 24–27), English Regency (*see* pages 28–29), Greek Revival (*see* pages 32–33), and Biedermeier, a less pompous and more functional version of French Empire, popular in Austria and Germany from ca. 1829.

All of these styles incorporated architectural and decorative elements that rendered them distinctive from one another. For example, English Regency accommodated motifs and imagery that were derived from the Gothic and Oriental vocabularies of ornament, whereas French Empire did not. Similarly, French Empire was predominantly Roman-inspired, while Regency employed both Roman and Greek ornament. However, because of the manner in which the styles drew heavily and reasonably accurately on Roman or Greek prototypes (or on both), they can be viewed as part of a coherent Neoclassical movement. The same cannot be said for many of the Classical revivals fashionable in the second half of the 19th century.

From ca. 1840 to the beginning of the 20th century, Classicism retained a powerful hold on the imagination of architects, designers, and the public alike, but it faced strong competition from a Gothic Revival characterized by historically accurate

Above **A fusion of delicate Adamesque moldings and a grander, Empire color scheme lies at the heart of the Federal-style interiors of Homewood House, built 1802–6 in Baltimore, Maryland.**

re-creations of Medieval styles of architecture, ornament, and decoration. Moreover, this "battle of the styles" between Gothic and Classical was echoed in an ongoing rivalry between markedly different styles of Classicism. Notable examples included a Renaissance Revival (*see* pages 12–13), loosely inspired by both Italian palaces and French châteaux of the 16th century, and a Baroque Revival (also *see* pages 12–13), which became known as Second Empire style in France and the United States, and which employed architectural detailing, motifs, and imagery similar to the original Baroque of the 17th century. A Rococo Revival that was based on the flamboyant, 18th-century French Rococo style (*see* pages 16–17) also proved popular, although it was variously, and somewhat confusingly, described as "Old French," Louis XV, or "French Antique"–imprecise labels that generally reflected the very loose interpretation of the original style.

This eclectic mix of Classical Revival and Gothic styles, which also extended to various, and somewhat heavy-handed, reworkings of earlier 19th-century Neoclassical styles, culminated during the last three decades of the 19th century in a widespread fashion for combining the different styles. It was not unusual, for example, to encounter a Neoclassical, Pompeiian-style hallway, a Gothic-style dining room and library, a Louis XIV drawing room, and a Rococo-style parlor all under the same roof.

Left The Flagler Mansion was built in Palm Beach, Florida, at the turn of the 19th century. Its architects, Carrère and Hastings, were heavily influenced by Neoclassical buildings and by the French Renaissance châteaux of the Loire.

Above The Neoclassical-style Waverley Mansion was built in 1852, in Columbus, Mississippi. Its cavernous octagonal entrance hall, or rotunda, is connected to the cantilevered balconies and a cupola above by a sweeping double staircase.

Above German architect and artist Karl Friedrich Schinkel redesigned Charlottenhof for Crown Prince Frederick William of Prussia in 1826. The Prince's study is lined with some of his extensive collection of copper engravings. The soft terra-cotta pink of the walls is subtly contrasted with the green, gray, and silver moldings– a color scheme that was inspired by Pompeiian decoration.

Left The large hall at Charlottenhof is a celebration of Neoclassicism. Features include watercolors based on frescoes by Raphael, a statue of David, a Roman-style lantern, and a console table with lion's head posts and Etruscan-style stretchers of anthemia, *paterae*, and scrolling foliage.

ELEMENTS OF
GREEK REVIVAL STYLE

The Greek Revival, a strand of Neoclassicism, made a major impact on European architecture and interior design from the 1780s to the 1840s, and proved equally influential in the United States from the 1820s to the 1850s. The sources of inspiration were the buildings and artifacts of Ancient Greece, many of which were unearthed in late 18th-century archaeological excavations on mainland Greece and in southern Italy. Initially, the Classical Greek vocabulary of ornament was combined eclectically with Roman forms and motifs, as in Adam style (*see* pages 22–33). From this,

however, emerged a purer Greek Revival, more strictly based on the original Greek Doric and Ionic Orders and on early Greek and Etruscan decoration and artifacts. Notable architects and designers working in this style included Sir John Soane (England), Benjamin Latrobe (United States), and Karl Friedrich Schinkel (Germany). The room shown left is in Neu Hardenberg, a Greek Revival house near Berlin, Germany, designed by Schinkel. Architecturally and decoratively, it displays the purity, refinement, and austerity of both form and ornament characteristic of Greek Revival interiors.

1. In grander Greek Revival houses, it was not unusual to have domed ceilings in some rooms, and, as here, coffered (compartmented) flat ceilings in others. The compartments could be formed by plaster or papier-mâché moldings, or, often, by painted decoration. Early 19th-century pattern books show a variety of fashionable designs for central ceiling medallions and borders consisting of *guilloche* (interlacing circular bands) and rosettes (as here), as well as combinations of other Classical Greek motifs such as acanthus leaves and anthemia. Dentil (squared toothlike) moldings were also popular, as on this cornice, as were Greek keys.

2. Medallions, trophies, and wreaths inspired by Greek originals were employed extensively as wall decorations in Greek Revival interiors. Favored subject matter depicted in medallions included winged horses (such as Pegasus), nymphs, and the female companions of Dionysus (the Greek god of wine and fertility).

3. The admiration for the essential simplicity and gravity of Greek architecture and ornament that characterized much of the Greek Revival is evident in these large, relatively plain wall panels. Embellished only with corner rosettes, they are in marked contrast to the more frivolous and convoluted grotesque panels employed in Adam interiors (*see* pages 22–23).

4. Contrasting shades and colors are employed to enhance the sense of three dimensionality and emphasize the configurations of the door paneling, and to tie it in en suite with the panels on the walls.

5. Schinkel and other architects working in the Greek Revival style made considerable use of the rather severe, masculine Greek Doric Order. The top of this fluted Doric column is embellished with a festoon consisting of fruit and flowers, and *bucrania* (the skulls of sacrificial animals, such as rams, oxen, bulls, or goats). Although a

symbol of fertility, *bucrania* were often omitted from Neoclassical festoons because of their association with sarcophagi and other funerary objects.

6. Vases and urns–either original, or more usually reproductions of Classical Greek and Etruscan wares unearthed during archaeological excavations in Greece and southern Italy–were among the most prominent decorative artifacts displayed in Greek Revival interiors.

7. Similar to French Empire and English Regency designs, these chairs display an abstract simplicity of form that ultimately has its origins in the slab-backed, saber-legged, armless *klismos* chair of Ancient Greece.

8. Archaeological excavations in Greece and southern Italy also provided a wealth of source material for the geometric pattern marble, tiled, and wooden parquetry floors favored in Greek Revival houses.

MODERNISM &
POSTMODERNISM

The late 19th-century fashion for Classical Revival interiors (*see* pages 30–31) endured on both sides of the Atlantic during the first three decades of the 20th century. Notable examples, mostly confined to grander houses, included Neo-Renaissance and Neo-Baroque (*see* pages 12–13), Adam-style (*see* pages 22–23), and Louis XVI (*see* pages 18–21) revivals. However, from the mid-1920s until the end of World War I, Classicism was over-taken in popularity, first by the Art Deco movement and then by Modernism.

Art Deco style was characterized by clean lines and smooth planes in walls, ceilings, floors, and wood-work, by contrasting-colored walls and woodwork, and by the use of predominantly abstract and geometric motifs derived from the early 20th-century art movements of Cubism, Expressionism, Futurism, and Fauvism, and from native African and South American art. As such, Art Deco drew little or no inspiration from the Classical vocabulary of architecture and ornament. Modernism, however, did draw on the principles of proportion that are inherent in Classical architecture. What underpinned Modernism was a desire to render the home, in the words of the influential architect and designer, Le Corbusier, "a machine for living in." In practice

Above The 19th-century Biedermeier chair and chest in Michael Graves's house in Princeton, New Jersey, display a clarity of line and a fitness-for-purpose well-suited to 20th-century Late-Modern and Postmodern interiors.

this meant shunning the use of "unnecessary" fixtures and fittings, highlighting the industrial origins of modern building materials, furniture, and textiles, restricting the color palette to white, off whites, and pale hues, and emphasizing the quality and texture of the materials used, rather than their embellishment. Where decorative motifs and patterns were used, they tended to be abstract, geometric, and Cubist-inspired, although Classical ornamentation such as coin molding, fluting, and wave-scrolls was employed.

Perhaps not surprisingly the second half of the 20th century witnessed a rejection of Modernism's unremitting rationality and minimal use of color and pattern–a development accompanied by the Postmodern "rediscovery" of Classical ornament and decoration. On the one hand, this resulted in the restoration of many post-Renaissance Classical interiors to their former glories. On the other hand, many Postmodern architects, designers, and decorators, who were engaged in the invariably inventive recoloring and patterning of previously plain, unornamented, Modernist architectural shells, began to use architectural fixtures and fittings, fabrics, furniture, and artifacts that were either directly modeled on, or inspired by, Classical originals.

Right Classical
references figure large
on this fireplace wall,
designed in 1984 by
Michael Graves for
Charles Jencks's colorful
Postmodernist residence
in London, England.
The columns over the
mantel supporting
Classical-style busts are
faux marble, as are the
fireplace and the fluted,
columnar side-tables.

Left The entrance hall of a house
in Sussex, England, designed in
1985 by John Outram, reveals how
the Postmodernist "rediscovery"
of Classical ornament has often
manifested itself in the enrichment
of wall surfaces with contrasting
colors and textures. Conceived
to a horizontal, rather than to a
vertical esthetic, dark red stucco–
polished with a hot iron to resemble
marble–is alternated with bands
of burr elm veneer edged with
aluminum. (The X-frame stool is
inspired by Greco-Roman models.)

Above In this apartment in Paris,
France, which was designed by
Yves Gastou, a Le Corbusier-style
solid-balustrade staircase rises
from a double-height sitting room
to an open gallery above. The
opening up of the internal space
is characteristic of many
Modern and Postmodern
interiors. Classical-style ornament
is evident in the bas relief on
the stairs, the geometrically
patterned floor (the carpet is
by Jacques Despierre), and the
bronze statuette.

EXTERIORS

POSTMODERNISM HAS DONE MUCH TO REAWAKEN OUR

APPRECIATION OF THE CLASSICAL REPERTOIRE. INDEED,

"NOW...IT HAS BECOME THE FASHION TO DECLARE THE

MODERN MOVEMENT DEAD.... THERE MAY BE, ONCE

AGAIN, SOME POINT IN DISCUSSING ARCHITECTURAL

LANGUAGE.... FROM SUCH SPECULATIONS THE CLASSICAL

LANGUAGE OF ARCHITECTURE WILL NEVER BE FAR FROM

ABSENT. THE UNDERSTANDING OF IT WILL SURELY

REMAIN ONE OF THE MOST POTENT ELEMENTS IN

ARCHITECTURAL THOUGHT."

(SIR JOHN SUMMERSON, 1988)

EUROPE

Right (above) Camberwell Grove was built 1770–80 in south London. It is typical of 18th-century English Classical terraces (row houses) in which adjoining houses were defined by alternating stucco and brick facades.

Far right Built from 1767 to 1775 in Bath, England, the curving Royal Crescent by the architect John Wood the Younger illustrates the more ambitious and stylistically unified Classical terrace fashionable during the mid- to late 18th century.

Right (below) Based on a design by Palladian architect Colen Campbell, Marble Hill House was built from 1724 to 1729 near London. Its proportioned facade is typical of early 18th-century Palladianism.

The one element that binds Palladian, Adam (or Neoclassical), and Regency styles together is the adherence to Classical precepts of proportion, arising from the idea that if the architect or builder applies a set of mathematical rules to the plans of a building, then beauty will result. The "rules" of proportion, as introduced by Lord Burlington, were based on the writings of the 16th-century Italian architect, Andrea Palladio. In turn, Palladio's theories were based on those of the Ancient Roman architect Vitruvius, who equated architecture with geometry, and built according to its rules, employing the square, the circle and, in particular, the cube. Introduced ca. 1714, the basic Classical style—now commonly known as Georgian in England—held sway for nearly 130 years.

Far left (above) Built 1811–28 in Regent's Park, London, John Nash's Cumberland Terrace fueled a fashion for fully stuccoed Classical facades that endured until the mid-19th century.

Left Many early 19th-century architects adapted the established forms and proportions of Classical facades. At Sir John Soane's London house, built from 1792 to 1824, Classical Greek ornament appears as incised linear motifs.

Far left (below) Osborne House on the Isle of Wight, England, was built 1845–61 to the designs of Thomas Cubitt and Prince Albert. Its campanilelike towers and arcading were inspired by Italian Renaissance palazzo.

The Palladian era was the first to popularize the terrace (row house), which was a practical choice for growing cities as it maximized building land and also suited the formalized plans of admirers of the Classical style. The first terraces had been built in the 1630s by the architect Inigo Jones in London's Covent Garden, but Classicism developed the terrace further, treating it not as a repeating pattern but as a design entirety, adding a central pediment, pilasters, and end projections to create the "palace front." By the mid-18th century terraces were being built in squares, circuses, and crescents; by the second half of the century, terraces began to be ornamented with ribbons, swags, and arabesques, first devised by Robert Adam for the Adelphi, a group of palatial houses on the Thames River in London.

Many eighteenth-century houses were built of brick, but Classical taste dictated that buildings should be faced in stone. This was financially feasible for grand houses, but lesser homes needed a more economical alternative. Thus builders began to use stone-colored brick, or they applied stucco (a thin cement or plaster based on lime and sand) to the facades and scored it before it dried to imitate blocks of stone. By the 1780s, Coade stone was also in widespread use. A ceramic rather than a stone, it could be cast to make key stones–a typical design was ornamented with a face in carved relief, plaques, statuary, and monuments.

The key feature of Classical architecture was the fenestration of buildings, that is, the placement and arrangement of windows. The double-hung sash was the quintessential Georgian window in England and Holland, but it never displaced the casement window in Europe. Classical style demanded that windows should be placed symmetrically on the facade of a building, and that within each window there should be a symmetrical arrangement of panes– six-over-six (six panes each on the top and bottom window) and eight-over-eight were the standard at first, and then, as larger panes became technologically feasible, four-over-four and two-over-two.

Above The 16th-century Villa La Rivella, near Venice, Italy, was designed by Andrea Palladio. Its entrance portico is derived from Ancient Roman temple fronts, rather than from original Roman villas.

Left The Villa Mansi was built in the 17th century in Lucca, in Tuscany, Italy. Its theaterlike facade, interspersed with ornament based on human figures, is typical of Baroque architecture.

Above The characteristic curves of Rococo architecture and ornament dominate the exterior of the Château de Morsan, a Louis XVI summerhouse built ca. 1736, in Normandy, France.

The door was the centerpiece of Classical-style buildings, and had to be positioned exactly central to the facade. The doors tended to be plain, perhaps only paneled in proportion, but the architectural detailing on the door frames could be highly elaborate, with columns and pilasters on either side, and decorative pediments. Later, the fanlight above the door became a decorative feature, and it also served to allow light into the hallway. In the 19th century the doors became more elaborate–studded doors in the Ancient Roman style were popular for a time–and the door frames became plainer, although they still featured Classical details.

Regency style, as espoused by the Prince of Wales (later King George IV), was a variant on French Empire and was interpreted in Britain by Sir John Soane and John Nash. Greek motifs such as egg-and-dart and Greek key joined familiar Roman forms, and lent buildings a severe line. Ancient Egyptian motifs, popularized by Napoleon's campaign in that country, brieflycame into vogue. Also fashionable was cast ironwork, a less expensive alternative to wrought iron, which was used for railings, light brackets, verandahs, and balconies. The most popular designs were derived from Classical motifs, from anthemia on balconies to small urns on railings.

Left From the Renaissance to the turn of the 19th century, landscaped parks and formal gardens have been a feature of Classical-style palaces and grand houses. This miniature maze, overlooked by a balustraded stone walkway, is at the Château de Courance, near Fontainebleau, France.

Left The Villa Pisani, near Venice, Italy, was designed by Francesco Maria Preti in 1736 during the European Palladian Revival of the early 18th century.

Right Neoclassical architecture became highly fashionable in Sweden during the late 18th and early 19th centuries. This temple-like pavilion stands in Haga Park, Stockholm, which was laid out by Fredrik Magnus Piper.

THE UNITED STATES

Above Designed by William Jay and built ca. 1816 in Charleston, South Carolina, Patrick Duncan House is a mixture of Neoclassical English Regency style and early 19th-century American Palladian Revival. Its pedimented portico is supported by Composite columns.

Right Featuring a prominent temple-front portico in which the emphasis is more on form than applied detail, the exterior of Richard Jenrette's house on the Hudson River in New York State represents the robust variant of early 19th-century American Classicism that is often labeled Roman Revival.

Classical style's heyday in America is divided into two eras: before and after the Declaration of Independence in 1776. The period prior to this date is generally known as the Colonial or Classical Georgian era. After 1776 American architecture is referred to as Federal, but this encompasses various Classical styles—Adamesque, emerging in the 1780s and 1790s, Palladian Revival (Jeffersonian), running almost concurrently with Adamesque, Neoclassical, mostly French inspired, and Greek Revival, the latter coming to prominence during the 1830s and 1840s. In the 18th century, America looked to Europe, particularly Britain, for inspiration, and joined with its enthusiasm for Classical style. It was only as the new Republic gained confidence that its architecture began to diverge in significant ways.

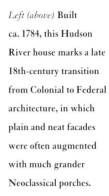

Left (above) Built ca. 1784, this Hudson River house marks a late 18th-century transition from Colonial to Federal architecture, in which plain and neat facades were often augmented with much grander Neoclassical porches.

Left (below) Teviotdale, in Linlithgow, New York State, was built just before the Revolutionary War and is a fine example of late-Georgian architecture. Notable features include the Palladian window above the entrance portico.

Below The White House in Washington, D.C. was designed by James Hoban and built between 1793 and 1801. Its facade was based on a design in the *Book of Architecture* (published 1728) by James Gibbs, the famous Scottish architect.

The overseas influence was a result of four factors: many wealthy Americans had taken the Grand Tour, and had first-hand experience of Europe; European pattern books, which were widely available, showed how to design and build in the Classical style; and the 18th-century building industry relied very heavily on immigrant British-born designers and craftsmen, which meant that new trends spread to America almost as quickly as they did to the British provinces. Also, in deference to the Classics, Americans sought to follow the ideals and architecture of Ancient Greece and Rome. One visible result of this was the classically inspired municipal building—from the White House to the local capitols—whose dome, rotunda, and portico are reminders of the prevalence of Classical taste.

The Colonial period is characterized by the influence of the British Georgian style, and so by 1740 the urban settlements of the east coast–Boston, Philadelphia, and Charleston–exhibited the symmetrical facades and sash windows of the genre. Brick was being used for facing buildings in towns, and housing was constructed in terraces (such as Philadelphia's Society Hill, begun in 1750). Country houses were built with the typically Palladian Venetian window (in which a central arch is flanked by two pedimented rectangles). As America was composed of immigrants, pure Classical style was mixed with and complemented by their influences. Regional differences grew with the population: Southerners designed their houses to maximize air circulation, while New Englanders found that the austerity and understatement of Palladian design suited their region's climate and character. Local materials were used pragmatically: if the pattern book showed a carved design, it was often executed in the far more plentiful wood, rather than in the stone used in Europe. Some houses–for example, Mount Vernon, the house built for George Washington, the first American President–were even faced in wood, cut and painted to look like ashlar (stone) blocks. However, Classical forms were still the basis for buildings both big and small.

Left Architect David Whitcomb built his house overlooking the Hudson River between 1983 and 1987. Classical inspiration is evident in the temple-front portico, and in the rotunda–the top of which can be seen projecting above the pediment of the portico.

Above The home of Ulysses S. Grant was designed ca. 1860 in the Italianate style. Derived from the rural Renaissance architecture of northern Italy, the Italianate is characterized by a low, pyramidal roof, with overhanging bracketed eaves.

The lighter, more graceful Neoclassical Adam style crossed the Atlantic in the form of pattern books during the Revolutionary War, and by the 1780s it had become the first look of the Federal era. The dining room of Mount Vernon, designed in 1775, is thought to be the first true example of Neoclassical style in America, but it became a very influential style at all levels of society, resulting in elongated windows, decorative cornices, and more airy rooms.

By the end of the 18th century, American architecture started to develop its own style. Pattern books originating in America began to be published, and classically trained architects were now shaping the way cities looked. The first great native-born architect—also the third President—Thomas Jefferson was enomously influential, and gave his name to a new form of Classicism. Jeffersonian style reverted to an appreciation of the ancient civilizations, and of form rather than employing the intricate detailing of the Neoclassical adherents. Although Jefferson was largely responsible for grand buildings (notably the University of Virginia, the Virginia state capitol, some Federal buildings in Washington, D.C., and his own home, Monticello), his influence was pervasive, as was his desire to "improve the taste of (his) countrymen."

Right and below Michael Graves's house in Princeton, New Jersey is a converted warehouse built in 1926 in Tuscan vernacular style. Covered in pink stucco, it is scattered with Classical references, including buttresses *(below)*, and a small outdoor courtyard *(right)* topped by a Palladian-style, semi-circular thermal window.

INTERIOR DETAILS

While key architectural fixtures and fittings, such as doors and windows, fireplaces, staircases, floors, and decorative moldings, were subject to various stylistic developments since the Renaissance, both their form and the manner in which they were employed in Classical interiors was always underpinned by a common philosophy of design: "Proportion is the first Principle, and proper Appropriation of the parts constitutes Symmetry and Harmony." (Robert Morris, 1751)

DOORS & WINDOWS

Right The practice of decorating door panels with pasted-on paintings, prints, and engravings emerged in the mid-18th century. Usually, the walls of the room—a print room—were embellished in the same manner. This decorative convention endured well into the 19th century and was particularly popular in England, Ireland, France, and the southern states of America. However, these paintings of imaginary architectural ruins by Manolo Morales are in a house in Madrid, Spain.

Right This pair of white-and-gilt, three-paneled doors in the living room of a New York apartment was designed by its owner, Bernd Goeckler. The applied motifs are all derived from the Neoclassical vocabulary of ornament. The winged figures in the lower door panels, and the Pegasuses (winged horses) on the frieze above, were especially favored in late 18th- and early 19th-century Empire style—the source of inspiration for the overall decorative scheme of the apartment.

During the later years of the Renaissance, the Medieval-style, battened-plank door was widely superseded by the basic framed and paneled wooden door characteristic of Classical interiors. Variations, which had architectural door frames of differing complexity, incorporated between two and six panels, usually square or rectangular, or sometimes curved, notably during the Rococo period. From the early 18th century the panels were often fielded (raised); from the early 19th century, they have sometimes been made of glass. Although they were mostly hung singly, double doors were often employed between adjoining reception rooms, with sliding doors being used in the United States. Glass-paneled French doors and internal louvred shutters were also in evidence, the latter serving as screen doors in hotter climates during the summer.

The grandest of doors were made from finely figured hardwoods, such as mahogany and rosewood. However, softwood doors were more common. These were either grained or painted, the panels and moldings often emphasized with gilding or in contrasting shades or hues.

Before the 18th century, most windows were either mullions (with fixed vertical bars) or transoms (with fixed horizontal and vertical bars). Grand houses also featured tripartite Venetian windows with a central arch top. Internal shutters were common and remained so until the late 19th century. However, from around 1700, counter-weighted, vertically sliding sash windows became prevalent. These has six, eight, nine (in the United States), or twelve panes of glass to each sash. Single-paned lower sashes came into vogue from the mid-19th century, while thin, delicate bars to hold glass in place were used in the late 18th and early 19th centuries.

Left Framed by Neoclassical pilasters, friezes, and cornices, the Music Room windows of the Nathaniel Russell House, built in 1808 in Charleston, South Carolina, are internally shuttered to offset the light, heat, and humidity of summer.

Above The windows of Homewood House in Baltimore, Maryland, are typically early 19th-century Neoclassical in style in their juxtaposition of simple glazing bars and large panes of glass with elaborate surrounds and drapes.

51

MOLDINGS

Left Neoclassical moldings provide an authentic backdrop for the early 19th-century Empire-style decoration and furnishings in Bill Blass's New York apartment. Of particular note is the dentiled (squared toothlike) cornice, which is embellished with rosettes, and bands of egg-and-dart (oval-and-V shapes) molding. The latter is also used to define the perimeters of the fielded paneling. A further feature is the pair of truncated columns with reeded moldings. Flanking the window, each is used to used to support a Classical-style bust.

Left Decorated in Directoire style by Borja Azcarate, this library in a Spanish apartment features a dentiled cornice and a room divider that is based on a late 18th-century model. The latter incorporates columns and other rectilinear moldings in keeping with the austere, pared-down Neoclassicism that is characteristic of Directoire style. The carved *flambeaux* (torches) under the arch at the top of the divider symbolize knowledge and enlightenment in Classical ornament, and thus have often been employed in studies and libraries.

Decorative moldings have always played a fundamental role in Classical interiors. Indeed, in *The Grecian Orders of Architecture*, published in London in 1768, Stephen Riou observed that "they compose the alphabet of architecture." On a practical level, moldings are usually applied to any junction between adjacent surfaces that needs to be disguised and/or elaborated. Typical examples include cornices (between walls and ceilings), baseboards (between walls and floors), and architraves (between door frames and walls). However, moldings are also applied simply to embellish otherwise plain surfaces. Notable examples include plaques and paneling on walls, coffering on ceilings, entablatures over doors, and fluting on columns and pilasters.

The simplest moldings are rectilinear, and are derived from the capitals, entablatures, and bases of the Classical Greek and Roman Orders (*see* pages 10–11). They are shaped in profile into various curved or angular forms; concave, convex, and right-angle profiles are the most common, and are often combined within a single molding. The architectural names for the best-known examples are ovolo, fillet, astragal, scotia, torus, bolection, ogee, cavetto, and cyma recta and cyma reversa. More elaborate rectilinear examples are made up of (and are also named after) a series of repeated shapes based on commonplace or decorative objects. These include dentil, egg-and-dart, bead-and-reel, cable, coin, ribbon-and-rosette, and Greek key moldings, many variations of which were devised after the Renaissance. To these can be added a wide range of moldings consisting of motifs or formal patterns that are based on decorative artifacts or on floral, faunal, mythological, and human forms. These include acanthus leaves, anthemia, palmettes, lotus flowers, husks, scrolling foliage, festoons, and wreaths; sphinxes, griffins, phoenix, and dolphins; nymphs, mermaids, and satyrs; and trophies, masks, vases, and urns.

Before the mid-18th century, techniques of building construction required many moldings, notably internal pilasters, corbels (brackets), and cornices, to play both structurally supportive and ornamental roles. As a consequence, moldings were made of substantial materials such as stone and wood. However, new building techniques introduced in the mid-18th century diminished the structural role of moldings. Thus, lighter materials, such as plaster and papier-mâché, were increasingly favored—a development that also resulted in Neoclassical moldings made of these materials becoming generally flatter in profile and more delicate in appearance than their Classical Greek and Roman counterparts.

Above **The curved panels on the Château de Morsan's original gilt and blue-gray door is typical of mid-18th-century French Rococo.**

Left **In contrast to Rococo-style curves, the Chinese yellow and gold walls of the Music Room at the Château de Morsan incorporate rectilinear paneling and fluted pilasters based on the Classical Orders. (The column is faux marble.)**

Right **Late 18th-century Neoclassical decorations at the Château de Compiègne include gilt anthemia and *pateras* (oval or round decorated dishes) on faux marble pilasters.**

FIREPLACES

Left This 17th-century Italian fireplace is in an apartment in Paris, France, designed by Yves Gastou. The dentil (squared toothlike) moldings under the mantelshelf, the carved scrolls on the frieze, and the pairs of reeded pilasters (parallel moldings on the columns) are typical of Baroque-style ornamentation. The Classical-style bas relief above the mantelshelf is by Alfred-Auguste Janniot, and was produced for the Palais de Tokyo in Paris, ca. 1940. The pair of French bronze and crystal candelabra also dates to the early 1940s.

Left This 19th-century Spanish marble fireplace features Classical acanthus-leaf carvings on its jambs and spandrels (triangular sections around the arch). Installed in the chimney is an iron salamander–a stove named after the mythical beast that resembles a newt or a lizard and symbolizes fire. The mirror above the fireplace was devised by Borja Azcarate, who decorated this apartment in Madrid. It consists of a 19th-century mirror glass set into a zinc window frame– the latter salvaged from a 19th-century French mansard roof.

After the enclosed wall fireplace superseded the Medieval open hearth at the start of the 16th century, the fireplace, and particularly the mantelpiece, became the dominant architectural feature and focal point of the Classical room. Except in some Modernist interiors, it has retained that status to this day, largely due to the suitability of its parts to Classical ornamentation.

Notable features included jambs (vertical sides) in the form of columns, pilasters, caryatids, and herms (male deities); marble or tiled slips (the strips that are set into the fireplace); friezes embellished with medallions, rosettes, scrolling foliage, urns, lyres, swags, cameos, or mythological scenes; mantelshelves edged with Classical moldings; and overmantels that incorporate mirror glass or paintings.

The most prestigious mantelpieces were carved from white statuary or colorfully veined marble, or porphyry (a variegated stone); sandstone, limestone, slate, granite, plaster, scagliola (imitation marble), hardwoods, cast iron, copper, and steel were also used. From the 17th century, mantelpieces that were made from pine, painted to resemble marble or finely figured hardwoods, were less costly alternatives.

STAIRS

Left Part of Bill Blass's collection of 18th-century model staircases is displayed on this Edwardian library table in his New York apartment. It includes two winding, closed-string newel staircases *(left and center left)*, a cantilevered, open-string, double-sweep staircase *(center)*, and a closed-string, balustered, spiral staircase *(right)*.

Left The principal staircase in Sir John Soane's House, built from 1792 to 1824 in London, England, is cantilevered and open-string. It incorporates plain and suspended rosette balusters of cast iron, a faux mahogany handrail, and a black-and-gold faux marble wall-string. Its red-and-gold, flame-and-leaf pattern stair runner is secured with brass stair rods.

In classically designed houses, the main staircase is usually a showpiece. Popular types include the straight flight, the dogleg (two parallel flights with a landing in between), winding (or curved) stairs, spirals (with steps that wind around a central column called a newel post), flying stairs (with steps canilevered from the stairwell without a supporting newel), and double-returns (which start with one flight and return in two). Pre-18th-century staircases were mostly closed-string, their balusters (the vertical supports for the handrail) set on a diagonal frame enclosing the stairs; the open-string, with its balusters fixed into exposed stairs, was widely favored thereafter. The materials included stone (often marble), polished oak or mahogany, painted or grained fir or pine, iron, and, for balusters, brass.

Although they were often round, square, or tapered, the balusters and newel posts were also shaped as columns, vases, and human and animal figures, or embellished with Classical ornamentation such as strapwork (decorative interlaced strips), acanthus scrollwork, wreaths, and Greek key patterns. Typical stair coverings included full-width carpet or central runners, painted floorcloths, and matting.

FLOORS

Right The entrance hall, like other rooms in Frédéric Méchiche's apartment in Paris, France, has been decorated and furnished in late 18th-century Directoire style. The octagonal-and-square stone-tiled floor is not original, but it is typical of the fashionable geometric patterns of the period. It was deliberately laid slightly unevenly to simulate the settling that would have occurred naturally over time if the floor had been installed in the 1790s.

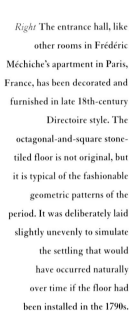

Right A marquetry marble floor graces the entrance hall of this Parisian apartment designed by Yves Gastou. The geometric pattern and the contrasting-colored marbles are typical of early 19th-century Neoclassical hallways and reception areas. Other Neoclassical-style elements include the pair of French Empire mahogany and leather stools, a Neo-Etruscan vase, an early 19th-century marble column (with a bronze figure), and painted-panel wallpaper.

Butt-jointed wooden boards were the most widely adopted form of flooring in non-reception rooms above entrance level in houses built since the Renaissance. Before the mid-18th century, the flooring was often made of oak or elm, but thereafter fir or pine were used. The latter also became increasingly common under carpets, rugs, floorcloths, or matting at ground level from the late 18th century onward.

However, since the 16th century, the most prestigious forms of flooring in entrance halls and reception rooms on any story were multi-colored stone flags or tiles, mosaics, hardwood marquetry and parquetry, and exotically veined marbles. Favored laying patterns ranged from simple herringbone or basket-weave repeats to the more complex geometric (and sometimes illusionistic) patterns that were derived from Classical archaeological sources. Where the cost of such flooring was prohibitive, less expensive options could be used. These included stenciled softwood boards, faux marbled or woodgrained floorcloths and linoleum, and cement-based simulations of mosaic, marble, or stone.

DECORATIVE ELEMENTS

CHOOSING A PERTINENT COLOR SCHEME AND SUITABLE

FABRICS AND WALLPAPERS IS AS IMPORTANT AS

ASSEMBLING THE APPROPRIATE FURNITURE, PAINTINGS,

AND OTHER DECORATIVE ARTIFACTS WHEN CREATING A

CLASSICAL-STYLE INTERIOR. HOWEVER, YOU SHOULD

ALWAYS BEAR IN MIND THAT "DECORATION AT ITS BEST

IS A GAME. PLAY IT WITH PANACHE, AIM FOR GRAND

THEATRICAL STATEMENTS, AND ALWAYS AVOID WHAT

OSBERT LANCASTER SO WISELY CALLED 'THE FATAL

WILL-O'-THE-WISP OF PERIOD ACCURACY'."

(STEPHEN CALLOWAY, 1990)

COLOR

Left The paneled walls of the Swedish Room, the main bedroom in Lillian Williams's Château de Morsan, built cá. 1765 in Normandy, France, are painted glacial blue and white. This color combination, which was prevalent in 18th-century Swedish Rococo interiors, is echoed in the painted French Rococo table and in the upholstered chair and firescreen.

Left Teviotdale is a Classical Georgian-style house built just before the Revolutionary War of 1775, in Linlithgow, Colombia County, New York State. The dining-room walls have recently been painted lavender which, like milky yellows, deep pinks, and shades of terra-cotta, stone, and gray, was a fashionable color in the United States during the late 18th and early 19th centuries.

Before the late 17th century, polychromatic color schemes were the height of fashion in Classical interiors. Rich primary reds, yellows, and blues, and various shades of green and brown, were much in evidence, with pigments derived from earth, clays, vegetable matter, metal oxides, and other materials such as ox blood, cattle urine, and beetle juice. While darker colors, particularly "drabs" (muddy browns and greens), remained in widespread use during the first half of the 18th century, they were gradually superseded by a lighter color palette that originated in the white-and-gilt reception rooms of French palaces of the late 17th century. By the mid-18th century, this had filtered through to English, European, Scandinavian, and American households.

Apart from white, paler and brighter colors favored during the late 18th century included pinks and light terra-cottas, pale greens and blues, pearl gray, and straw, pale citron, and Chinese yellow. More vivid alternatives included violet, turquoise, pea green, and cerise. Underpinning this new esthetic was a growing understanding of color theory via works such as Moses Harris's *The Natural History of Colours* (1766), which explained how to mix over three hundred tints from fifteen basic colors, and also helped decorators to employ various shades of the same basic color on adjacent flat and molded surfaces to emphasize subtly the architectural proportions and details of a room.

Light colors, especially pearl white, pale pink, lavender, and, in the United States, bright blues, greens, and yellows, remained generally fashionable until the 1840s. However, partly due to the invention of aniline dyes, richer and more vivid colors came back into vogue during the middle of the 19th century. Typical examples, which remained popular in many households until the end of the century, included sharp yellows, deep blues, acid greens, crimson, purples, and mustards, and earthy reds and browns, the latter enlivened by being juxtaposed with gold or yellow.

A late 19th-century reaction to these strong, vivid hues came in the form of ivory, pale gray, and other stone colors, "greenery-yallery" (olive green), milky yellows, hyacinth blue, and "old rose." This lighter palette set the tone for the white and off-white color schemes of Modernist interiors, and the paler colors, such as buff, beige, coffee, eau de nil (Nile green), and pastel blues and pinks, that have been popular since the 1930s. These have proved fashionable for much of the 20th century, and have only been challenged in Classical interiors by the Postmodernist Revival of some of the darker, pre-20th-century period color schemes.

Right Bill Blass painted the walls and ceilings of his New York apartment in shades of off white to provide a neutral backdrop for his collection of early 19th-century furniture, including a George II armchair and a Regency side cabinet.

Left Rich shades of red on the walls, upholstery, and carpet contribute to the opulence of the Music Room in Richard Jenrette's American Empire-style house on the Hudson in New York State.

Below Color schemes became lighter around the mid-18th century. The shades of yellow in this 1760s' English living room are typical of the period.

WALLPAPERS & FABRICS

Right The trompe l'oeil wallpaper in the hallway of the Morris Jumel Mansion, in Harlem, New York, is a documentary reproduction of the original bought in Paris in 1826 by the wife of the owner. Known as "Colonnade," it is produced in pale yellow and two shades of gray, and features festoons at frieze height, colonnades in the field, and a variety of Neoclassical motifs at and below the dado.

Right Designed and decorated in Swedish Gustavian style by Borja Azcarate, this living room in a Spanish apartment prominently features a pair of Louis XIV-style armchairs. Their frames are painted gray to complement the walls, which are painted in stucco—while the plaster is still wet. The chairs are upholstered in a cotton fabric embellished with hand-painted monograms and Classical-style foliate borders.

Until 1740 walls were paneled, and then painted; afterwards the fashion, primarily in Europe, was to hang the field (the central part of the wall) with tapestry or silk brocade, stretched and fixed onto wood strips, while paneling or plastering the dado (the lower part of the wall). Wallpaper gradually became popular, and was either stuck directly to the wall, or fixed onto the wood. The latter meant that papers could be taken with you when you moved—a practical alternative because wallpaper was a luxury even for the wealthy, paper was scarce, and printing was done by hand using wooden blocks. Wallpaper designs imitated earlier wall treatments, such as plasterwork or, most commonly, textiles. Flock wallpaper—where powdered wool was applied to paper bearing a glue "pattern" to create the illusion of a cut-pile fabric, usually damask—became fashionable in Classical interiors in Europe and America. In England the textile hangings in the Great Drawing Room at Kensington Palace, home of George II, were replaced by flock. Stripes were popular, as was self-colored silk, which alternated shiny and matt (then known as tabby). By 1760, repeating

Right **This Regency daybed in Bill Blass's New York apartment features a carved lion's head on its frame and is covered with a striped fabric. Striped silk, linen, horsehair, and cotton fabrics were very fashionable during the early 19th century, and were initially inspired by the striped bunting hung from the exteriors of French houses in order to celebrate Napoleon's military victories.**

Classical motifs—arches, urns, statuary, niches—on wallpaper became widespread; these were sometimes supplied with a "relief" pattern made with papier-mâché for a trompe l'oeil effect. The French led the way in wallpaper design and production, and their imitation of fabric on paper created the fashion for matching textiles and wallpapers.

Textiles increasingly played a role in Classical interiors, progressing from plain to elaborate. Early fabrics—velvet, damask, wool—were heavy and were regarded as a utilitarian feature of the room. Later, a lighter look prevailed, and silk—plain, watered, taffeta, damask patterns—became the fabric of choice. A late 18th-century vogue for cotton and cotton chintz (inexpensive and quick to produce because of the Industrial Revolution) did not displace silk, and its supremacy was reasserted when Empire style came into fashion after the turn of the 19th century. This highly decorative interpretation of Classical style made widespread and patriotic use of French silks, particularly in golden yellow, bright green, crimson and white satin, woven with Imperial motifs. Fabric swathes and festoons were intrinsic to the look, typified by tented rooms, where silk was draped or pleated over all four walls, and often the ceiling too.

Left **The Regency mahogany chair in the Owen Thomas House, in Savannah, Georgia, is upholstered with a gold-on-red silk. The pattern combines anthemia motifs with a floral garland and scrolling foliage.**

Right **The living room at Plas Teg, a Jacobean house in North Wales, is decorated in Regency style. Furnishings include a George IV chaise longue, a striped brocade fabric on the walls, and an Aubusson carpet.**

FURNITURE

Right **The 19th-century mahogany four-poster bed in a Greek Revival house in Charleston, South Carolina, has been left undraped. During the latter part of the 19th century it became fashionable to remove heavyweight fabric hangings from four-posters in order to improve the air circulation in bedrooms, particularly in hotter climates. However, in regions where mosquitoes and other insects were a problem, lightweight sheers, such as organza, muslin, and lace, were often draped from the rails running between the tops of the corner posts.**

Right **Improved upholstery techniques during the 18th and 19th centuries resulted in a substantial increase in demand for ever-more comfortable seating. The French daybed in this apartment in Paris, France, designed by Yves Gastou, is a typical example, with its generous button-back mattress, plump, tasseled bolsters, and loose cushions. Classical embellishments of the frame include animal hooves and stylized foliage motifs, the latter echoed in the floral pattern of the early 19th-century Aubusson carpet and in the carvings on the fireplace.**

Beds and Couches

Many beds favored in post-Medieval, Classical interiors were modeled on Greek or Roman originals. Seventeenth-century daybeds and late 18th- and 19th-century *lits-en-bateau* (boatlike beds) were inspired by Greek *kline* (beds used for reclining while eating, and also for sleeping) and its Roman equivalents, and had plain or carved animal legs, a footboard, and a headboard decorated with silver inlay and bronze mounts.

Other beds were not strictly Classical in form, their designs having evolved after the decline of the Roman Empire. However, these beds did incorporate structural components and decorative embellishments, such as columns, cornices, and motifs, derived from the Classical repertoire. These included canopied and draped four-posters; *lits à la duchesse* (with just head-posts, supporting a half-length canopy); *lits d'ange* (postless, with a "flying" canopy suspended from the wall); and *lits à la polonaise* (their domed canopies hung from a central corona secured by rods curving up from the bedposts).

Left A Federal side-chair, made ca. 1810 in New York for Nathaniel Russell House, in South Carolina. The chair's saber legs, lyre back, striped silk pillows, called squabs, and painted anthemia are Neoclassical.

Right This mahogany-framed, silk-upholstered, Federal récamier (ca. 1815) has rosette, anthemion, and scrolling foliage brass mounts.

Below A Second Empire mahogany armchair. Its red silk upholstery features laurel wreath and palmette motifs.

Chairs and Settees

Like beds (*see* pages 72–73), many types of seating found in Classical-style interiors were developed after the decline of the Roman Empire. Chairs with upholstered seats appeared in the late 16th century; loose pillows were used prior to this. Upholstered wing armchairs, settees, and sofas were introduced in the late 17th century. Many new styles of chair-back were devised in the late 18th century—a golden age of furniture-making that was characterized by the use of numerous finely figured hardwoods, such as mahogany and rosewood, and by carved, ormolu, gilded, painted, and wood, ivory, and brass inlay decoration. Notable 20th-century innovations included the utilization of materials such as plywood, tubular steel, aluminum, and plastic.

Nevertheless, in terms of both basic form and decorative embellishment, many chairs owed much to the wooden, marble, and bronze "prototypes" of Ancient Greece and Rome. Greek examples included the *diphrros okladias* (a cross-legged stool, with carved animal feet); the *thronos* (with carved rams' heads at the arm-ends, and a back that is often shaped either like a snake or a horse's head); the *klismos* (armless, with inwardly curving legs and a horizontal, curved back-support); and the *kline* (*see* page 72). Roman examples include variants of the *klismos* and X-frame stool; plain, wooden-paneled chairs; stately armchairs that are carved with animal or caryatid figures; and setteelike benches with both the backs and the arms decorated with painted or inlaid motifs.

Tables

Left Carved animal legs, husks and *patera* motifs, and a marble top are features of this French Empire console table in an apartment in Paris, France, by Yves Gastou. The Neoclassical vases are the urn are inspired by Greek prototypes.

Below Made by Gilbert Poitterat in 1940, this table has a forged-iron base, with X-frame stretchers based on sinuous, scrolling plant forms. These are joined by a wreath–a symbol of sovereignty, honor, and glory in Ancient Greece and Rome.

Most of the hardwoods and decorative embellishments employed in the manufacture of chairs (*see* pages 74–75) were also used for the production of tables in Classical-style interiors. For example, mahogany, walnut, and rosewood veneers, marquetry inlay tops, and carved legs and feet, were especially prominent. However, materials such as marble, slate, bronze, and iron were also utilized, particularly for those tables inspired by original Greek and Roman models. Notable examples included small tables with round or rectangular tops of bronze or silver, and bronze or wooden legs with carved animal feet; large, rectangular, marble-topped dining and serving tables with carved marble legs or end-supports; and *mensa lunata (*half-round console tables) on curved legs.

Chests, Closets, and Cabinets

Although often lavishly decorated, Ancient Greek, Etruscan, and Roman storage furniture was fairly basic. The Greeks, for example, had no closets, and used wall-hooks, open shelves, or wooden chests. The latter had painted or inlaid hinged lids and paneled sides, and legs that ended in lion-paw feet. Similarly, the Etruscans used circular bronze chests engraved with figures and supported on paw feet, while the Roman equivalent was a boxlike chest embellished with inlay and bronze or silver mounts. However, under the Roman Empire, closets with shelves and doors were introduced, the most elaborate examples in the form of armoires with architectural components such as flanking columns and carved pediments.

Some items of storage furniture used since the Renaissance were modeled on these early pieces, notably *cassoni* (marriage chests), wine coolers, and various types of wardrobe. However, many new forms were also devised, including chests of drawers, chests-on-chests, chests-on-stands, and linen presses for clothing; bureaux, escritoires (fold-down desks/cabinets), davenports (desks with side drawers), and pedestal desks for writing and storing papers; numerous types of bookcase; and sideboards, chiffoniers (pedestal cupboards with shelves and doors), and other storage and display cabinets. Mostly constructed from polished hardwoods, or painted or grained softwoods, these pieces, when designed for Classical interiors, have a commonality that resides in their display of moldings and motifs derived from Classical ornament.

Left This imposing Biedermeier secretaire, made in southern Germany ca. 1820, now resides in Bernd Goeckler's New York apartment.

Right The secretaire in this apartment in Paris, France, designed by Yves Gastou, is the work of the Italian designer Piero Fornasetti. Made in 1950, it is decorated with images derived from Classical architectural prints and engravings. The trompe l'oeil effect on the lower section is typical of Fornasetti's chic and witty furniture designs.

Left In a Parisian apartment designed by Yves Gastou stands this double-door cabinet designed ca. 1940 by André Arbus. Made from sycamore, it is embellished with Classical motifs and imagery, and features carved volutes (scrolls) on the tops of the square-tapered legs. These scrolling forms were originally the main component of the capitals of columns employed in the Ionic Order of architecture, and are said to derive their shapes from the horns of a ram.

MIRRORS

Left The *girandole* (convex) wall mirror first appeared in France during the middle of the 18th century, and by the early 19th century had become highly fashionable in other European and in American interiors. This example is in a house in Madrid, Spain, and features foliate (carved leaves), bead, and gilt ball moldings on the frame. In France, England, and America, more elaborate versions were often crested with an eagle. Flanking snakes that supported candle sconces were also favored in English Regency interiors.

Left This mid-18th-century wall mirror in Brian Juhos's apartment in London, England, has an ornate giltwood frame incorporating carved C-scrolls and S-scrolls, and is further embellished with acanthus leaves and *caulicoli* (stalks). All are derived from the Greco-Roman vocabulary of ornament, although those seen here are inspired by the more elaborate Roman versions. Often employed on mirror frames in Classical Revival interiors, they were especially favored by designers working in the Rococo style.

Mirrors featured very prominently in Classical interiors, and served, through reflection, to enhance the natural and artificial lighting of a room and to increase the sense of space. Before the late 18th century, mirror plates were mostly made from blown glass–a process that limited their size and rendered them the preserve of the wealthy. Thereafter, the perfection of casting techniques (initiated by the French in the 1690s) facilitated the production of less expensive and larger plates. Fashionable types of mirror included overmantels above fireplaces; chevals (dressing mirrors); pier glasses (hung between windows); and wall mirrors–the most popular shapes being rectangular, oval, round, cartouche (scroll-shaped), and convex. Framing materials included gold, silver, copper, plaster, and, most commonly, wood–the latter often gilded or painted. Styles of frame ranged from simple rectilinear moldings, to pedimented columns inspired by the Classical Orders, to elaborate sculptural compositions incorporating geometric, mythological, floral, and faunal motifs that were derived from Classical ornament.

COLLECTIONS

Right The diverse range of decorative objects displayed in Frédéric Méchiche's recreation of a late 18th-century townhouse in his Parisian apartment is testament to the internationalism and eclecticism of his taste in art and ornament. Here, a late 18th-century Italian marble-top console table plays host to a collection of African tribal masks, an arrangement of rock crystals, and a gilded Louis XVI model clock case in the form of Classical ruins. (The painting is by Francis Bacon.)

Right Of particular note in Peter Hone's extensive collection of Classical architectural fixtures and fittings are a Coade stone eagle ca. 1810, numerous plaster casts displaying diverse Classical motifs and imagery, and a large Coade stone urn (also ca. 1810). On a marble-top, white-painted oak table by George Bullock (behind the eagle) stands a ball finial by William Kent on a Coade stone balustrade, and an early 19th-century sarcophagus copied from a Roman original.

The Grand Tour

While extensive collections were assembled in Rome as early as the 16th century, the fashion for collecting Classical antiquities only became an international phenomenon following the advent of the Grand Tour of Continental Europe in the late 17th century. This cultural treasure hunt, which began with the aristocracy and an esthetic elite, expanded to accommodate the newly affluent middle classes, and increased tourism in the 19th century, still survives in the auction rooms, antique dealers' showrooms, and architectural salvage yards of today. As early as the mid-18th century, the demand for souvenirs easily outstripped the availability of original artifacts unearthed during the archaeological excavations at Herculaneum and Pompeii in Italy. Collectability, then and now, thus extends to what Mark Twain artfully described as "authentic fakes and forgeries" of original fixtures and fittings and ornaments, and to post-17th-century commemorative paintings, sketches, maps, metalwares, ceramics, and glass.

poncirus trifoliata

Statuary and Obelisks

The vast majority of statues, obelisks, columns, and other diverse architectural fixtures and fittings, dated to Classical antiquity and unearthed during the archaeological excavations in Italy and Greece during the 18th and 19th centuries, are now in museums. Therefore, most private collections, even those first accumulated in the mid-18th century, are made up of Neoclassical copies either cast from, modeled on, or simply inspired by the originals.

Among the most popular and affordable collectables are the models of Classical temples, columns, and ruins made during the late 19th century, either as souvenirs for tourists or as study tools for students. Rarer 18th-century examples are even more sought after, primarily because they display more intricate detailing—a quality reflected in their price. The best are carved from alabaster or from exotically veined yellow and red marbles, such as *rosso antico*. Cork models were also produced, but these were prone to drying out and crumbling, so very few of them have survived.

A tremendous variety of ornamental moldings was cast from original excavations in the 18th and 19th centuries. Typical fixtures and fittings included friezes, entablatures, pediments (low-pitched gables), cornices, jambs, key stones (central stone in an arch), capitals, and diverse individual motifs. As with the architectural models, 18th-century examples are generally rarer and of better quality than 19th-century equivalents—factors again reflected in their price.

Left **Peter Hone's plaster figure of Apollo, the Greek god of the sun and patron of music and poetry, is probably French and dates to ca. 1860. Apolline decoration has been employed extensively in Classical interiors since the Renaissance.**

Above **The entrance hall of a Parisian apartment designed by Yves Gastou plays host to a 19th-century marble sculpture of an angel, by Piero Calvi. Angels were often used as personifications of Victory in Roman ornament.**

Most expensive, but perhaps most evocative of Classical antiquity, are the Neoclassical sculptures of figures and busts that were produced in considerable quantity to meet huge demand, especially during the second half of the 19th century. Among the most highly prized are full-length figures by sculptors such as Sir Alfred Gilbert, William Henry Rinehart, Chauncey B. Ives, and Hiram Powers—the latter an entrepreneurial American who, like many fellow artists of various nationalities, established his studio in Italy on the route of the Grand Tour during the mid-19th century.

While 18th- and 19th-century life-size sculptures commanded high prices at the time, and are astronomically expensive today, most artists produced more affordable busts. Also, in 1828, Benjamin Cheverton, the sculptor, invented a machine that produced small-scale, identically proportioned, and relatively inexpensive copies of life-size figures, and these became available to meet the burgeoning demand of shallower pockets. Notable subject matter, made in marble, bronze, Coade stone, Parian ware, or plaster, included gods such as Apollo, Eros, Aphrodite, and Circe, mythological characters such as Icarus, and numerous anonymous male and female figures. Of the latter, the most sought after (then and now) was Hiram Powers's *Greek Slave*, of which he produced some one hundred variations in the 1840s. Full-length versions are now all in museums or private collections, but it is still possible to purchase one of the busts.

Left (above) Grouped on a painted Carlos IV-style marble-top table in Borja Azcarate's apartment in Madrid, Spain, are *(from the left)* a table lamp mounted on an 18th-century Spanish polychrome (multicolored) column; an anonymous female figure in alabaster; a 19th-century Italian alabaster bust of Dante Alighieri; a 19th-century alabaster urn; a "topiary art" iron ball (intended as a garden ornament); and a pair of 19th-century alabaster vases.

Left (below) A pair of herms (male deities) supports the top of a marble console table in Peter Hone's apartment in London, England. The table was recently found in a coal cellar in London's Euston Road, not far from Thomas Hope's house in Portland Street. Hope (1769–1831) was a highly influential patron of the arts with an extensive collection of Greek, Roman, and Egyptian artifacts, and it is possible that he may have once owned this table.

Right This superb Classical Roman torso is carved from white statuary marble. It stands in the corner of Bill Blass's New York apartment, which he remodeled and furnished in late 18th- and early 19th-century Neoclassical style.

Above **Nineteenth-century floral-patterned, hand-painted, and gilded glass bowls and plates (of English and Hungarian origin) grace the Regency dining table in Brian Juhos's London apartment.**

Left **These 19th-century Swiss Nyon porcelain cups and saucers have typical 18th-century Classical decoration, including floral swags and silhouette medallions.**

Right **This pair of Italian Neoclassical porcelain vases, with painted and gilded decoration, was designed by Gio Ponti in 1940.**

China and Glass

Inspired by the discoveries of Ancient Roman, Greek, and Etruscan pottery in Italy and Greece during the 18th and early 19th centuries, most of the European pottery and porcelain factories produced wares—jugs, urns, vases, pitchers, bowls, plates, cups, and saucers—either copied from or inspired by original Classical forms, or simply decorated with Classical imagery. Particularly collectable are the pieces made by Worcester, Coalport, Minton, Spode, and Rockingham in England; by Vienna, Sèvres, Meissen, and Copenhagen in Europe; and by William Tucker and Charles Cartlidge in the United States. Of special note are the Etruria (Etruscan) vases and Jasper cameo wares of Josiah Wedgwood. Most are faithful to the original Classical forms, and the Jasper wares are highly distinctive. Produced in base colors of pale cobalt blue, sage and olive green, lilac, lavender, black, or yellow, they display Classical scenes in crisp white low relief.

Equally collectable is the 18th- and 19th-century glassware made in imitation of Roman originals by Thomas Webb, W. H. and B. & J. Richardson, Stevens & Williams, Joseph Locke, and the Mount Washington Company. Notable types included cameo glass with mythological scenes cut in opaque white relief over darker base colors, such as cobalt blue; mold-blown vases, bottles, flasks, and jugs—green tinted, blue, purple, or amber and either square or rectangular, or in the shape of heads, fruits, or animals; and everyday drinking glasses engraved with Neoclassical imagery.

Above **These prints and engravings in a Spanish apartment feature motifs and imagery derived from the Classical vocabulary of ornament.**

Right **This group of 19th-century Classical-style vases was compiled by Yves Gastou.**

Far right **Paintings and prints of Ancient Roman and Greek buildings became fashionable following the archaeological excavations of the 18th century. These examples are owned by Frédéric Méchiche.**

Prints and Pictures

The practice of decorating reception-room (rooms for entertaining) walls with fine art collections depicting Classical ruins and architectural studies of locations on the Grand Tour, or of scenes from Classical Greek and Roman mythology, was widespread during the 18th and 19th centuries. However, oil paintings by leading artists such as Pompeo Batoni, Sebastiano Conca, and Antonio Canaletto were almost exclusively the preserve of the aristocracy. Fortunately, during the early 18th century an alternative and less expensive decorative convention emerged when it became perfectly acceptable, rather than just financially expedient, to collect and hang framed prints and engravings.

By the mid-18th century, this practice had been taken a stage further with the fashion for decorating entire rooms with collections of prints pasted directly onto painted or papered walls and sometimes doors. Initially popular in England, Ireland, and France, print rooms also appeared in the grander American houses, particularly in the southern states, during the late 18th century, and remained in vogue well into the 19th century. In many cases, black-bordered black-and-white prints were simply pasted up in regimented rows, often on straw-colored backgrounds. However, more flamboyant arrangements, such as those conceived by Robert Adam and Thomas Chippendale, incorporated trompe l'oeil paper cutouts of Classical bows, swags, garlands, and chains "supporting" and embellishing the prints.

THE CLASSIC ROOM

THE CLASSICAL VOCABULARY OF DECORATION AND ORNAMENT OFFERS GREAT SCOPE, AND, HISTORICALLY, DOES NOT NECESSARILY DEMAND UNIFORMITY THROUGHOUT ALL THE ROOMS OF A HOUSE. FOR EXAMPLE, "IN SO FAR AS STYLE IS CONCERNED THE MODERN FRENCHMAN DWELLS IN THE 18TH CENTURY, HE SLEEPS IN THAT CENTURY LIKEWISE, BUT HE DINES IN THE 16TH, THEN ON OCCASION HE SMOKES HIS CIGAR AND ENJOYS HIS COFFEE IN THE ORIENT, WHILE HE TAKES HIS BATH IN POMPEII, IN ANCIENT GREECE."

(JACOB VON FALKE, 1873)

HALLS

Right The hallway of a Parisian apartment designed by Yves Gastou is lined with Classical columns and pilasters. The linear symmetry of the space is emphasized by a pale-colored stone floor divided by contrasting black borders. An Egyptian sculpture is displayed on the stone column at the end of the hall. Following archaeological excavations in Egypt and North Africa in the late 18th and early 19th centuries, Egyptian artifacts became very fashionable in Neoclassical interiors.

Right The mahogany doors opening onto the staircase landing of this Parisian apartment designed by Yves Gastou are embellished with painted Neoclassical motifs and imagery (dated to 1810). A stone statue from Classical antiquity stands next to the 20th-century iron balustrade designed by André Dubreuil. Other features of note include the 20th-century glass and forged-iron lighting fixture by Eric Schmitt, and the wall-hung French tapestry, which dates to the 15th century.

The 18th-century hallway was a public area, where guests came and, perhaps, waited for a short time; as such it was vital to give a good impression of the owner's taste and style, and to demonstrate the basic precepts of Classicism—proportion, symmetry, and order.

Overall the look was plain and subtle. A solid floor of pale Portland stone, interset with small diamonds of a black stone (usually slate or marble) was highly prized and a hardwearing status symbol. However, as most houses were built with wooden floors, those who sought

to follow the Classical style would often paint them to resemble stone, particularly marble.

Decoration often featured the shallow moldings that had been popularized by Robert Adam. The festoons and the garlands Adam favored were later developed into many kinds of Classical imagery, including acanthus and laurel leaves, medallions, urns, rams' heads, sphinxes, griffons, and curling arabesques. By the second half of the 18th century, complete sets of these ornaments were available in England and the United States from French catalogs. Often made

Left This Spanish hallway was decorated by Manolo Morales in late 18th-century Carlos IV style. Classical columns flank the doors. The hall floor is Carrara marble; the bathroom floor is Spanish mosaic. The painted decoration is inspired by Neoclassical Italian imagery.

Right The walkway in David Whitcomb's house in New York State encapsulates the monumentality, symmetry, and coolness of 18th-century Classical interiors.

Below The painted faux marble floor and faux stone-block walls in this New York hallway are redolent of 18th-century Neoclassical interiors.

of papier-mâché or sometimes of a gypsum mix, the ornaments were glued to the wall or attached with slip (liquid plaster) for an "instant" Classical look.

Other furniture and accessories were kept to a minimum. A console table—often with a semicircular top supported by a single decorative scroll-shaped bracket—was a popular choice on which to display a selection of treasures, perhaps a pair of urns flanking a statue or bust, with the objects always arranged in perfect symmetry. Pedestals bearing busts or candelabra, scroll-back chairs placed against the wall, or floor-standing statuary were arranged to make a "statement," often more by their dramatic placement than by any intrinsic merit, and purely to please the visiting eye.

LIVING ROOMS

Left The living room in Bernd Goeckler's New York apartment is decorated and furnished in Neoclassical style. The predominantly pale yellow and light brown color scheme, enlivened with touches of gilding, is typical of late 18th- and early 19th-century interiors. Period artifacts include a Viennese giltwood and crystal chandelier ca. 1790–1800; an 18th-century Louis XVI writing desk; and, on the architectural column, an early 19th-century bronze and gilt candelabra.

Left A 19th-century blond-wood Biedermeier secretaire dominates one corner of a Parisian living room designed by Yves Gastou. The Neoclassical architectural detailing–columns, pilasters, pediments, and other linear moldings derived from the Classical Orders–is characteristic of Biedermeier furniture. Next to the secretaire is a Napoleon III armchair, which has been sympathetically re-covered in a stylized flower-and-leaf-patterned, petit point tapestry.

The living rooms of an 18th-century house were primarily designed to accommodate the social events of the time. In Robert Adam's plans for Syon House, the Duke of Northumberland's London home, which he remodeled in the 1760s, he describes a classically inspired interior which had to encompass both large rooms (for rendez-vous and entertainments and for receptions after dinner) and small rooms (where ladies withdrew).

Early in the century, European society was marked by its formality–a complex set of unspoken rules shaped the minutiae of every social

activity. This was echoed in the arrangement of what we now call living rooms, with furniture placed around the edges of the room. In the Classical tradition, low, backless couches, often with scrolled ends, were set against the walls, perhaps flanked by scroll-back chairs. On an outside wall, a console table with a pier glass over it might be positioned between each window.

By the turn of the century, although the furniture styles were still inspired by Classicism, the arrangement became more informal; furniture was brought forward from its usual position

against the wall and left in the middle of the room permanently, known as *dérangé*. Pairs of couches were placed at right angles to the fireplace (which led to backs being necessary), and a greater desire for comfort led to advances in upholstery techniques and to more widespread use of upholstery on chairs. The sofa table, useful for holding books and needlework, was introduced, while occasional tables, which could be moved where needed, also became popular. The invention of the

Above Obelisks have been a recurring ornament in Classical architecture since Ancient Roman times. The mirrored obelisk in this Parisian living room by Yves Gastou was designed by Gilbert Poillerat.

Right In this drawing room by Yves Gastou, 18th-century paneling provides the backdrop for the classically inspired 20th-century chairs and stools by André Arbus, and for a table by Gilbert Poillerat.

Left Inspired by late 18th-century Directoire style, this living area in Frédéric Méchiche's Parisian apartment features a Napoleon III satin-upholstered sofa.

Right Another living area in Frédéric Méchiche's apartment is furnished with a white-painted Empire settee signed by Janselme.

Below Frédéric Méchiche salvaged the white-painted wall-paneling from late 18th-century Parisian houses. The sofa is Italian and dates to ca. 1800.

Argand lamp–a more efficient kind of oil lamp–in the 1780s meant that several people could share the same light source, so it became fashionable to gather around small lamp-lit tables in the evening, to play cards or talk.

These changes did not diminish the popular taste for Classicism. The archaeological excavations at Herculaneum and Pompeii in Italy in the late-18th century inspired many new styles, including a craze for the colors found among the ruins–lilacs, blues, greens, pinks, and black. Panoramic wall decorations, often featuring idealized landscapes inspired by Classical murals, were briefly fashionable, but by the early 1800s most stylish walls were decorated in a Grecian-inspired two-dimensional scheme, with bold borders and a discreet repeating pattern based on Classical motifs. This was either done freehand (for the wealthy) or stenciled. A theme of terra-cotta red (or Pompeiian red) and black, named after the Ancient Etruscan pottery on which it was first seen, became particularly fashionable.

Empire style, although born in France in the 1790s, is closely associated with the Imperial phase of Napoleon's career (from 1804 to 1815). It became popular in the rest of Europe and in the United States, where it was followed by the more austere Greek Revival, which tended to emphasize form and shape rather than ornament. After Napoleon invaded Egypt in 1798, Egyptian motifs–winged lions, scarabs, lotus buds, obelisks, and sphinxes–became fashionable and appeared on everything from console table legs to lamp bases. Many of these images also appeared as statuary or

Left Furnishing and artifacts in Bernd Goeckler's New York living room (also shown on page 98) include a pair of Le Corbusier black leather and chrome armchairs; an Empire-style German daybed of ca. 1800; and a bronze figure of a Roman gladiator (copied from the marble original discovered near Rome in 1611).

Below This living room by Yves Gastou is furnished with a 1950s' Aubusson carpet on a parquet floor; a 1940s' André Arbus sofa; a pair of mirrored obelisks, and a marble-top table with an S-scroll, forged-iron base by Gilbert Poillerat; and a collection of Neoclassical-style bronze sculptures.

objets d'arts, and their arrangement–especially in pairs–in perfect symmetry was the height of taste. The manner in which pictures were displayed, in geometric patterns, was as important as their subject matter (ancestors, views, landscapes, and Classical ruins). The centerpiece was usually a circular convex mirror, in a gilt frame ornamented with balls, or crested with an eagle, or flanked with snakes supporting candle sconces.

Curtains throughout the Empire period were lavish and elaborate. Early in the 18th century, festoon blinds (called *l'Italienne*) were used, but when Empire style became popular, pairs of muslin curtains were often surmounted by permanently fixed, elaborate, silk drapes, with a plain blind for shading the room. Napoleon singlehandedly rescued the ailing French

silk industry when he placed many large orders for furnishing silks. Golden-yellow satin became a central theme of Empire style, especially when adorned with the Emperor's symbol, the bee. Floors were covered with woven carpet, but it was usual to leave a band of wooden floor showing. Painted canvas floorcloths were also popular in England and the United States as, unlike wool carpets, they could be taken up and washed.

Above **This sitting room by Borja Azcarate has a canvas ceiling painted with Classical moldings and cupids. Other features include a faux marble-top table and a collection of Classical bronze figures.**

Right **The Classical symmetry and proportion evident in the furnishings and architectural shell of this room, designed by Yves Gastou, is underlined by a pair of wall-hung torchères–an Ancient Greek symbol of life.**

Left Bill Blass's New York living room is furnished in late 18th- and early 19th-century Neoclassical style. Apart from the dentiled cornice, features include a Regency daybed, a mahogany strip floor, and Classical columns and busts.

Above Also furnishing the 18th-century Parisian drawing room, decorated by Yves Gastou (shown on page 101), are pairs of forged-iron chairs and candle sconces by Gilbert Poillerat, and a green-lacquered cabinet by André Arbus.

LIBRARIES & STUDIES

Left The walls and ceiling of the study adjoining this Parisian library, designed by Yves Gastou, are draped with fabric to create the military-style, tentlike effect fashionable in 19th-century Neoclassical interiors. The library features bookshelves framed by mahogany columns, pilasters, and pediments derived from the Classical Orders. Nineteenth-century furnishings include a pair of animal-skin upholstered Directoire stools, French Empire mahogany chairs, and a geometric- and floral-patterned carpet.

Left The study in Brian Juhos's 1960s'-built London apartment has been furnished in early 19th-century Neoclassical style. The leather-topped, mahogany-and-gilt writing desk is Louis XVI style, and supports a 19th-century plaster statuette of Mercury, the Roman messenger of the gods. The mahogany-frame, upholstered desk chair is Russian Empire style and dates to ca. 1810. The carpet features a small motif repeat pattern and s simple linear border, often favored in early 19th-century interiors.

The library, which very often also served as a gentleman's study, became an integral part of the 18th-century house—for two reasons. A personal collection of books had become an aristocratic accoutrement as a result of most young gentlemen (although not young ladies) embarking on a formal education. Also, it had become fashionable for the eldest son to undertake the Grand Tour of Continental Europe to increase his level of sophistication and make an extended study of Classical culture. Those who had been on the Grand Tour—which meant anyone with means from England and the United States—came back with an appreciation of Classical style and a taste for the ideals of patronage. They also returned with the fruits of their travels—statuary, urns and vases, and decorative plaques. Some of these items, particularly in the early years of the Tour, were genuine relics thousands of years old, but most were bought in warehouses which supplied "souvenirs." Thus a private room was needed to house their volumes of the Classics and writings about them, and also give them a place to study and appreciate their collections.

The obvious style for furnishing such a library was Classical. Bookcases were the starting point, and were often designed as an element of the architecture, being built according to Classical precepts of scale and proportion and incorporating classically inspired moldings such as egg-and-dart or Greek key, columns, balusters, and perhaps topped with a broken pediment. The room was frequently painted in a deep, rich red, which was felt to be the best background for the display of pictures and objects. The curtains were heavy, sometimes with blinds to shield the treasures within from the fading effect of strong sunlight. This necessitated a selection of lamps for reading and study, and they too would become part of the classically inspired theme; usually they would bear heavy bases in the form of a sphinx or an urn. Busts of philosophers—Socrates or Plato— brought back from the Grand Tour would be displayed around the room for inspiration. Seating was usually at an imposing desk, with writing materials formally set out for correspondence and for keeping journals. Special furniture had to be developed for libraries—sets of library steps with which to reach the top shelves, for example.

As the 18th century drew to a close, and a greater sense of informality prevailed within houses, the library gradually became more of a room that the whole family could use. In effect it was transformed into a less studious room—once sofas, small tables, upholstered chairs and other comforts were moved in, and one to which company could be welcomed.

Above Fronting a collection of books on Classical architecture in Bill Blass's library *(right)* are 19th-century bronze statuettes of Ancient Greek and Roman wrestlers, athletes, and acrobats.

Below The chairs around the table in Frédéric Méchiche's library were originally made by Jacob Desmalter for the corridors of the great French palaces– Trianon, Versailles, and Fontainebleau.

Right Furnishings and artifacts in Bill Blass's library also include a Regency library table, X-frame Regency stools, fragments of Roman carvings, and three 6th-century B.C. Greek helmets.

DINING ROOMS

Left Eighteenth-century fixtures and fittings play host to 20th-century furnishings in this Classical-style Parisian dining room designed by Yves Gastou. The marble fireplace, parquet flooring, and green-and-gold paneled doors and wall-paneling are 18th century, the latter augmented with *grisaille* (monochromatic trompe l'oeil) panels of cherubs. The green-lacquered dining table, leather-upholstered chairs, and glass-fronted cabinet were designed by Gilbert Poillerat in 1940. The 1950s' chandelier, in the form of a stylized cactus (a Classical motif), is by Carlo Scarpo.

Left The 19th-century Classical-style artifacts in this Madrid dining room by Borja Azcarate include a plaster bust of a Roman head on the dining table and a pair of cast-iron urns on the radiator cover. The urns are topped by a pair of scrolling foliate forms made of zinc and salvaged from the exterior of a 19th-century building. The Louis XVI-style dining chairs are also 19th century, while the off-white, cream, and light gray color scheme has been established by wallpapers from Osborne and Little's "Sienna" and "Shagreen" collections.

In the 18th century eating and drinking were taken very seriously, and so the dining room was considered an important room in the house. The social conventions of the day dictated that the gentlemen spent a good deal more time at the table than the ladies.

Dining rooms were furnished in a somber style, with large, heavy furniture. Mahogany, which was imported from Honduras, was the favored wood in both Europe and the United States. Its suitability for carving made it a good choice for the more ornate styles and, being a larger tree, mahogany could be cut into bigger pieces, making it perfect for dining tables. Classical style manifested itself in the shape of the legs, which might feature lion's paw feet, popular in Empire style, or lighter inlays featuring a Classical medallion on more delicate tables.

To accommodate the seriousness of the dining experience, Robert Adam invented the sideboard. This was made up of a marble-top table, with an urn on a pedestal at each side. The sideboard was designed to hold all the necessities of a dining room, with the urns

Above **The detail of the table setting in the room shown** *left* **features a Classical-style bust of Queen Victoria, Fürstenburg and Davenport porcelain, and a tablecloth bearing Victoria's emblem.**

Left **Peter Hone's homage to Classical antiquity includes plaster casts of Classical figures, a Coade stone urn, and a bust of Lord Byron.**

Right **Classicism's symmetry, proportion, order, and ornamental subtlety are exemplified by the dining room of this Federal mansion on the Hudson River.**

containing water to rinse the wine glasses. Later versions of the sideboard had a warming-plate cupboard, which was metal-lined and incorporated a small heater–a boon in some houses, where the kitchen was some distance away from the dining room.

Decoration was quite restrained, with red being a popular choice of color. Curtains were impressive but not overly fussy, due to a belief that folds of fabric could harbor food smells. Later in the period the curtain pole and other non-fabric components of an elegantly dressed window–brackets, finials, rosettes, bosses (raised ornaments)–might be decorated with gilt and styled using Classical motifs.

As elsewhere in the house, the display of treasures was important, and appropriate to the dining room were fine examples of china–statement pieces drawing inspiration from the Classics. Wedgwood's Black Basaltware faithfully reproduced the styles and patterns of Ancient Roman and Greek vases, while Jasper cameo ware (the look that Wedgwood is best known for even today) bore delicate white Classical scenes and motifs on matt backgrounds colored in Roman-inspired lilac, blue, green, and black. Proudly displayed on brackets or columns might be Wedgwood's copy of the Portland Vase, a famous Roman piece from the 1st century B.C., or a piece of Worcester or Derby porcelain in a Classical shape and decorated with an idealized landscape scene. When it came to setting the table, Wedgwood's creamware would be particularly appropriate, with its simple Classical lines.

Above The dining room in Joan Thring's London house has been decorated and furnished in early 19th-century French Empire style. The painted division of the walls is highly characteristic of the style, as are the "leopardskin-" upholstered, cane-back dining chairs.

Right The breakfast room in Michael Graves's Princeton, New Jersey, house features block-paneled walls, inspired by the stone facades of 18th-century English townhouses. The carpet, the faux grained metal chair, and the pedestal table were all designed by Graves.

KITCHENS

Right **An early 18th-century Classical look is evoked in this late 20th-century English kitchen. The base cabinets feature raised and fielded panel doors, flanked on the sink cabinet by Palladian-style pilasters derived from the Corinthian Order of architecture. The gray-brown-green "drab" paint used on the cabinets is also reminiscent of the early 18th century. Enlivened with brass faucets and drawer knobs, it harmonizes with the teak worktops and the black-and-drab, faux marble, checker-pattern floor covering.**

Right **When designing the kitchen in his house on the Hudson River in New York State, David Whitcomb drew inspiration from the monumentality and rectilineal symmetry of Classical architecture, and tailored it to meet domestic requirements, such as the need for storage space. The 20th-century emphasis on textures and colors is evident in the harmonious juxtaposition of gray slate flooring, a block-concrete hearth, blond-wood veneered shelving, and off-white painted walls.**

Before World War I, the kitchen was a functional room and the realm of the servant, even in modest households. As a result, style was of little importance. Thus to create a "Classical-style" kitchen, it is necessary to invent one by selecting elements and using them in a modern-day context.

Fitted kitchen units are easy to design along Classical lines if the rules of proportion and symmetry are followed. The starting point is the column, which divides into base, shaft, and entablature. Cabinets can be made with an elaborate cornice top and bottom, and each pair

delineated with a molding in the shape of a baluster or column, or each door framed with reeded moldings. A black-and-white color scheme could feature a marble floor and festoon blinds in a monochrome print featuring Greek or Roman busts. An unfitted kitchen could have a mahogany linen press with a pedimented top, a glass-fronted cabinet to display a china collection in Classical shapes, and a marble worktop. These elements could be unified in the Classical spirit by a single color on the ceiling and walls–a neutral stone or an Etruscan terra-cotta.

BATHROOMS

Right The sink unit in this Spanish bathroom designed by Borja Azcarate consists of a travertine marble top applied to an early 19th-century Empire cabinet. The mirror, which is also 19th-century Empire style, is flanked by a pair of Azcarate halogen lamps made of convex glass set in iron frames. The lamps are embellished with leaf forms, which were a popular motif in Classical ornamentation. The coloring of the walls–gray and beige–is inspired by Pompeiian decoration.

Right Period authenticity permeates this 18th-century French Directoire-style bathroom designed by Frédéric Méchiche for a Parisian apartment. The faux marble, zinc-lined bathtub, which is original, is augmented with a pair of elegant, swan neck pillar faucets. The walls are also faux marble, and feature *grisaille* (monochromatic trompe l'oeil) landscape panels flanked by pilasters. Heating is provided by underfloor water pipes–as would have been the case in an original Roman villa.

In the 18th century, when the appetite for the Classical style was at its height, bathing was not an everyday occurrence. Before the advent of water that was piped directly to houses (the ability to pump water around the house, and particularly to the upstairs rooms, was not available until the 19th century), the drawing of water was tedious and time-consuming. Only the very rich had servants to heat the water and carry it up to an antechamber; for everyone else there was simply a jug and bowl on a washstand in a bedroom or anteroom, and a chamber pot.

However, some wealthy people not only began to have a private bathroom where they bathed frequently (not just in summer), but they also managed to achieve cleanliness with some style. Baths were often made of copper, with an inner lining of fabric to protect the bather's skin. French examples had a tentlike canopy that transformed the bath into a steam bath, and a stand which made it look like a daybed. Florentines bathed in ornately decorated baths with a scrolling top edge, which were filled by water that spurted from two lion's head faucets fixed to the wall.

A chair next to the bath concealed a bidet, which one writer said was for "baths of a special nature."

Bathrooms in private homes became more common in the Victorian period and had a Classical feel. Features included a marble floor in alternate black-and-white squares; a deep, scroll-edge, claw foot bath with a painted marble exterior; a porcelain basin mounted on a column pedestal; and tiles patterned with egg-and-dart and Greek key motifs. When they are used in today's bathrooms, they will evoke a Classical mood.

Left Classical-style furnishings in this bathroom by Manolo Morales include fielded wall-paneling; a free-standing bathtub; a basin on a column pedestal; a 19th-century tripod table; a Charles X chandelier; 18th-century Venetian mirrors; and Carrara marble flooring.

Above In contrast to the Classical eclecticism of the Spanish bathroom *left*, this minimalist bathroom, designed by American architect David Whitcomb, draws for its inspiration on those tenets of 18th-century Classicism: order, symmetry, and proportion.

BEDROOMS

Left An 18th-century *niche de chien* (dog bed) stands in a corner of one of the boudoirs in Lillian Williams's 18th-century Château de Morsan, in Normandy, France. The bed is draped in the style of the *lits à la polonaise* that were fashionable in 18th-century Rococo and Neoclassical interiors. The curtains, made from a striped French cotton fabric, are puddled (gathered) on the floor, a decorative convention chiefly associated with Classical interiors, and originally employed as a sign of opulence and wealth.

Left Heavily draped four-poster beds were often employed in Classical interiors during the 17th and early 18th centuries, but they fell out of favor during the late 18th and early 19th centuries, when they were usually replaced by half-tester (canopied) beds. However, the lightly draped, or undraped, four-poster enjoyed a revival during the middle of the 19th century. This mid-19th-century American bed is made of mahogany, and is covered with a silk organza bedspread to match the sheers used at the windows.

Some kind of room to sleep in relative privacy and comfort has always been a desirable feature in houses, but Classical-style interiors epitomized the height of luxury, ease, and relaxation. The most opulent was the bedroom designed for Madame Récamier in 1798 for her Parisian home. The centerpiece was a low black couch, with Classical gilt moldings, and scrolled ends, each bearing a gilded swan. As was the French fashion, the couch was placed with its side against the wall (the English style was to have the headboard to the wall). The bed-hangings were white Indian muslin, fringed and spangled in gold stars. Flanking the bed was a pair of night tables in black and gold, supporting a gilded sphinx.

Wealthy couples had separate bedrooms, and later in the century the lady's bedroom came to be known as a boudoir; it had a large bed to sleep in (in a curtained alcove) and a daybed (in a small niche) for reclining and receiving visitors. There were two main fashions in Classical-style beds. Both were ornamented with hangings, which were vital to keep out the drafts as much as for privacy. Four-posters were still common, but

Left This 18th-century French boudoir features a Louis XVI *lit à la polonaise,* with period hangings by Scalamandré, and a Louis XVI lyre-back chair by Georges Jacob.

Right Flanking the four-poster in Brian Juhos's Neoclassical-style bedroom are a Swedish Empire clock and an 18th-century marble bust of Augustus Caesar.

Below Engravings of Classical imagery are hung on the walls of this bedroom designed by Manolo Morales. The bed is Louis XVI.

the early fashion was for a *lit à la polonaise* (Polish-style bed), which was topped by a dome, held up by rods rising from the four corners of the bed, or attached to brackets fixed to the wall. Later the *lit-en-bateau* (boat-shaped bed) came into fashion; this, too, was draped with hangings suspended from a coronet.

Blue and white were the colors of choice—red was deemed too fierce, yellow produced an unpleasant reflection, and green seemed somber. There was a profusion of softening fabrics, gathered into a coronet or adorning the windows, and an immense scattering of cushions on the bed, daybed, and around the room.

Above **Furnishings and artifacts in Michael Graves's Postmodernist bedroom include a 19th-century Biedermeier chair and wrought-iron pedestal, and a copy of a Greek bust of Aphrodite from the 3rd century B.C.**

Right **Bill Blass's Neoclassical-style bedroom has a solid mahogany floor. The globe on the Edwardian mahogany table is 18th century. However, it is the 19th-century bronze figure of Napoleon on horseback that dominates the room.**

CASE STUDIES

WHILE THE RESTORATION OR RECREATION OF INTERIORS

TO A SPECIFIC PERIOD OR DATE IS CERTAINLY POSSIBLE,

"THE SENSE OF CLASSICISM CAN [ALSO] BE SUGGESTED

BY ECONOMICAL MEANS, AND MAY BE COMMENTED

UPON BY A VARIETY OF METHODS IN DESIGN. LIKE ALL

GREAT LANGUAGES WITH A HUGE VOCABULARY AND A

VAST RANGE OF EXPRESSIVE SUBTLETIES, [CLASSICISM]

IS NOT A MATTER OF MERE IMITATION: IT OFFERS

ENORMOUS POSSIBILITIES FOR EXPRESSION, CREATIVE

DESIGN AND COMPOSITION."

(JAMES STEVENS CURL, 1992)

HUDSON RIVER HOUSE

"The house is inspired by the symmetry, order, coolness, and sense of dignity inherent in Classical architecture.... And to further emphasize the continuity of the past to the present we combined humble modern materials, such as concrete blocks and MDF, with architectural 'tailings' salvaged from the iron mine and other old buildings."

DAVID WHITCOMB

David Whitcomb's new house was built 1983–87 on a ridge in the Catskill mountains, high above the Hudson River in New York State. The site was an old iron mine, working until 1859 and serviced by a now disused railway cut through the surrounding woods. In both its conception and its construction, Whitcomb was determined that the house reflected the historical significance of this location and demonstrated a continuity with the previous use of the site.

In planning terms, this took the form of a series of spacious rooms projected from the central spine of the building—

Above **A pair of weathered Greco-Roman-style stone busts standing on the table shown** *left* **instantly evokes the architecture and the ornament of Classical antiquity.**

Left **The concrete block walls of the covered walkway provide an appropriate backdrop to an altar-style table. Its faux fabric covering (made of metal) serves to disguise its primary function as a portable bar.**

a metaphor for the opening up of North America by the pioneers who cut, mined, and railroaded their way north, south, and west from the states of the Eastern seaboard. Similarly well-lit, by large windows and, in the case of the "external" covered walkway, a transparent roof, the interior of the house was opened up to the old frontier, rather than "white-picket-fenced" off from it.

Continuity with earlier constructions was achieved by the reuse of old materials, notably the slate-tiled kitchen floor, salvaged from a museum in Albany, New York State, and the ashlar (stone-block) masonry used to

build the front wall and portico, and salvaged from the ashlar piers that supported the old railway. These architectural "tailings" gave the house its name—Tailings, but to underline the link between the past and present, were combined throughout with modern building materials, such as concrete and MDF.

Stylistically, the architecture, the decorations, and the furnishings are predominantly Classical in its broadest sense. In other words, they draw inspiration

Left **In addition to a sculptured torso and a gilt mirror with a broken pediment, Classical references in the rotunda include a rusticated masonry door and window frames, a stone-block wall, and a geometric-pattern, faux-marble wooden floor.**

Above **In another part of the walkway, an 18th-century marble-top console table with animal legs and S-scroll stretchers sits under a gilt-frame mirror and supports a black *tondino* (round dish) and a pair of Neoclassical-style bronze candelabra.**

from a variety of Classical styles. For example, the ashlar- (stone-block) walled walkway evokes the monumentality of Classical Roman architecture, while the living room rotunda recalls both Ancient Roman and Italian Renaissance models. Also evident are 18th-century Palladianism in the rusticated masonry windows and door frames of the rotunda and Renaissance-style murals on the guest-bedroom walls. Painted faux stone and marble floors, Greco-Roman style statuary, and artifacts and pieces of late 18th-century French Neoclassical furniture complete a scheme that accurately reflects the eclectic nature of American Neoclassicism from the 18th century to the present day.

NORMANDY CHATEAU

"The château was built as a summerhouse, ca. 1765, towards the end of the reign of

Louis XV. The exterior, with its curving facade, is Rococo, but the interior

plan is more rectilinear and Classical in style. Full of secret doors and boudoirs,

I think of it as a 'folie d'amour'."

LILLIAN WILLIAMS

Lillian Williams's restoration and refurbishment of her home in Normandy, France, provides a fascinating insight into the development of French architecture and decoration during the second half of the 18th century. The Château de Morsan was built ca. 1765 as a *maison de plaisance* or summerhouse and, originally surrounded by forests, would have also served as a hunting lodge. Its facade (*see* page 40) incorporates the elegant, curving forms and delicacy of ornament typical of the French Rococo architecture fashionable during the reign of Louis XV (1715–74). The influence of Rococo decoration and

Above Used from Ancient Greek and Roman times, marble conveys an air of solidity, formality, and opulence. Here a Louis XV marble-top console table displays antique quills and seal-stamped documents.

Left The furnishings and the glacial-blue-and-white color scheme in Lillian Williams's bedroom are predominantly late 18th-century Swedish Gustavian style.

ornament is also evident inside the château, particularly in some of the furniture and soft furnishings. However, in terms of its general layout, its architectural fixtures and fittings, many of the color schemes, and the majority of the furnishings and artifacts, the interior is predominantly Neoclassical in style. In this respect it reflects the gradual move away from Rococo style to Neoclassicism (the *goût antique* or old style as it was called) in France under the reign of Louis XVI (1774–92).

The difference between the two styles is apparent in many of the architectural moldings used throughout the rooms. For

141

example, the curvaceous gilt-paneling of the glazed doors leading off the entrance hall recalls the Rococo, whereas the moldings on the walls of the entrance hall and in many of the bedrooms, and, especially, the pilasters in the Music Room, are more austere, rectilinear, and Neoclassical in profile.

Similar contrasts of shape and form are also inherent in the design and selection of the furniture. The yellow-silk-upholstered French daybed and the stools in the Music room—like the legs of the marble-top Louis XVI console table in the main bedroom—display the straighter, more restrained lines characteristic of late 18th-century Neoclassical pieces, while most of the beds in the château are *lits à la polonaise*. Introduced in France in the mid-18th century, named after Louis XV's Polish Queen, and a fashionable element of Rococo-style boudoirs, these beds feature domed fabric canopies that are held in place by curved, fabric-covered rods attached to the bedposts.

The fabrics selected by Williams for use throughout the château are also highly redolent of the changing fashions in French taste during the the second half of the 18th century—a subject and period on which she is an international authority. Around the middle of the century, exotic floral patterns inspired by the decorations on imported Chinese ceramics, and featuring flowers such as the chrysanthemum, were the height of fashion in Rococo interiors. However, during the third quarter of the century, these were gradually supplanted by less exotic, smaller, and more delicate flowers, such as

Above **Next to the Louis XVI chair in the entrance hall, terra-cotta cherubs are displayed on a Classical-style plinth.**

Left **Painted rectilinear wall-paneling embellished with interlaced foliage, a gilt-framed portrait, a marble bust, and a Louis XVI console table capture the essence of late 18th-century French Neoclassical interiors.**

Right **A Louis XV bureau occupies pride of place in the entrance hall and stands under a late 18th-century chandelier.**

roses, carnations, poppies, cornflowers, daisies, stocks, violets, and anemones. Many of these appeared on the fabrics used in the French Queen Marie Antoinette's boudoir in the Petit Trianon at the Palace of Versailles, and are echoed in the floral sprigs and repeated small floral motifs of the fabric hangings on many of Williams's *lits à la polonaise*. Also represented are the plain-colored and striped fabrics that became increasingly popular towards the end of the 19th century. Notable examples include the plain, vivid yellow window drapes and the red-and-yellow-striped stools in the Music Room; further examples of striped fabrics can be found on chairs in the entrance hall, in the dining room, and in some of the bedrooms.

Above The yellow, gold, and brown color schemes that are used in the Music Room were very fashionable in late 18th-century interiors.

Left Classicism has frequently embraced Egyptian imagery, such as this imposing Louis XV terra-cotta sphinx.

Right Oriental influence is often apparent, as seen in these hand-painted chinoiserie scenes on the 18th-century Italian harpsichord.

The color schemes Williams has chosen are also highly characteristic of late 18th-century Neoclassical interiors. The mauve-blues and greens in the entrance hall are typically French, as is the pale yellow (enriched with gilding) in the Music Room, and in one of the bedrooms (where it is contrasted with white moldings). However, the pale, more muted glacial-blue-and-white scheme in the main bedroom was inspired by Swedish Gustavian interiors. Neoclassical Gustavian style became popular in Sweden under the reign of Gustave III during the last quarter of the 18th century. Initiated by French architects and designers, it was characterized by a preference for symmetry, restrained ornamentation, and cool, pale colors, such as muted blues, pearl gray, and straw yellow, which were usually applied together to both the furniture and the walls.

L O N D O N   A P A R T M E N T

"I have always greatly admired late 18th- and early 19th-century Neo-classical

interiors. So, when I bought my 1960s' apartment up on the 20th floor,

I simply had to bring some of their elegance, and glamour, and

richness of ornament to modern tower-block (high-rise) living."

BRIAN JUHOS

Soon after the English interior designer Brian Juhos bought a small apartment on the 20th floor of a 1960s', concrete-built, central London high-rise, he began to receive messages of sympathy from friends and relatives. They had assumed that only a change of personal circumstances could have forced him into a bland, Late-Modernist high-rise that appeared to be the antithesis of his preference for Neoclassical architecture, decoration, and ornament.

Nothing, however, could have been further from the truth. The apartment was exactly what Juhos had been looking for. It offered extensive views over London and

Above **Among the numerous Neoclassical artifacts displayed in Brian Juhos's London apartment is this pair of late 18th-century French Directoire, gilt-bronze candlesticks.**

Left **The serpentine-backed sofa in the living room is American and made in 18th-century Chinese Chippendale style. Standing in front of it is a Russian Empire-style table dated to ca. 1810.**

beyond, with Kensington Palace, Hyde Park and, on a clear day, even Windsor Castle, in Berkshire, all within its field of vision. It also provided all the cultural and work-related advantages of a central London location and, because it was situated "up in the clouds" on the 20th floor, isolated Juhos from some of the disadvantages, notably the noise of rush-hour traffic. First and foremost, however, the blank canvas of a typical 1960s' interior gave him the perfect opportunity to demonstrate the viability of recreating the opulence and grandeur of a Neoclassical interior within a modern architectural framework.

Right Flanked by a pair of Louis XVI gilded chairs (only one shown), a Louis XVI commode stands below a William Kent-style gilded mirror. It supports a Chinese pot and Swedish Gustavian candlesticks, both 18th century.

Far right The chandelier above and the chairs around the Regency dining table are 18th-century Swedish; the gilded mirror is 18th-century English.

Below Standing on a Classical-style scagliola (imitation-marble) column is an early 18th-century French plaster bust of Marianne (a symbol of liberty).

Central to Juhos's remarkable transformation of the apartment has been the introduction of numerous fine-quality, 18th- and 19th-century furnishings and artifacts. English Palladian Revival, Louis XVI, Swedish Gustavian, French Directoire, French and Russian Empire, and English Regency styles are all represented. Their harmonious juxtaposition throughout the rooms is due partly to Juhos's skill in the art of "placement" (or positioning), and partly to the essential compatibility of pieces inspired by the shapes, colors, patterns, motifs, and imagery that lie at the heart of the Classical vocabulary of style and ornament.

Equally significant, however, is Juhos's treatment of the ceiling, walls, and floors–the architectural shell. The installation of a bold, dentil cornice (between the tops of the walls and the ceilings) instantly establishes a Classical setting. Similarly, the laying of fitted Brussels-weave carpet immediately evokes late 18th- and early 19th-century Neoclassical interiors, and underpins a predominantly blue, off-white, and gilt color scheme also highly characteristic of the period. Most ingenious of all is Juhos's employment of mirrored wall-paneling (augmented with antique, gilt-framed mirror glass) throughout much of the apartment. A decorative convention that has its origins in the famous *Galerie des Glaces*, designed for Louis XIV's Palace of Versailles during the 1680s, it serves to increase the sense of space, multiply and integrate the furnishings and artifacts, and, above all, magically enhance both the natural and candle-lit illuminations.

P R I N C E T O N   H O U S E

"The Classical ideal Michael Graves is committed to reinvestigating is reflected not only in the character of the architectural surround he has created, but also in the furniture and objects he has been collecting since 1960, when as a student at the American Academy in Rome he bought an Etruscan vase for five dollars at a flea market."

ELIZABETH SVERBEYEFF BYRON

The eminent American architect Michael Graves bought his house in Princeton, New Jersey, in 1977. The original building was an L-shaped warehouse that had been designed in 1926 as a furniture repository for Princeton University, and had been constructed by Italian stonemasons from hollow clay tiles, bricks, and stucco in Tuscan (northern Italian) vernacular style. Over nearly two decades, Graves converted the warehouse into his private residence and a showcase for his collections of furniture, pictures, and *objets d'art*, and its style reflects his own conversion to Classicism as the natural language of architecture.

Above Stone-block paneling in the stairwell provides the backdrop for a bronze torso–one of the numerous Classical references to be found throughout the Warehouse.

Left Framed by ebonized wooden columns, a Roman-style oculus (circular opening) in the second-floor rotunda allows light to pass from a transparent roof-top dome above through to the entrance hall below.

Trained in the Modernist tradition, Graves first came to public attention in the early 1970s as a member of the New York Five, a group of architects whose work was inspired by the white concrete, Cubist esthetic of the influential French architect Le Corbusier. However, by 1977 Graves had become disenchanted with the Modern movement, believing it to be an architectural language "based largely on technical expression...rooted in functionalism and abstraction," and "dominated by the metaphor of the machine." Graves also felt that "in its rejection of the human or anthropomorphic representation of previous architecture...in favor of nonfigural, abstract

Above The table in a window recess in the dining room is a 19th-century copy of a Pompeiian brasserie (small table). Like the Temple of Vesta inkwells around the statue's base, it was a popular souvenir of the Grand Tour.

Right Furnishings in the living room include a Biedermeier table and chairs, two Michael Graves studio-design easy chairs (one shown), a Kashmir chainstitch carpet, and a *grisaille* (monochromatic trompe l'oeil) wallpaper panel—the latter a reprint of Zuber's *Les Amours de Psyche* of 1816.

geometrics," Modernism had become "inhuman and unnatural." For Graves the way forward involved a recommitment to Classicism and, particularly, the reintroduction of "figural elements" into his work. This approach, which was partly inspired by the two years he had spent as a student in Rome during the early 1960s, established him as one of the founders of Postmodernist architecture, and has given new life and vigor to the Classical tradition.

Graves's particular commitment to Classicism is evident throughout his converted warehouse (now called the Warehouse), in which previously plain, unadorned Modernist surfaces have been enhanced with a variety of figural elements and other Classical

references. Notable examples include the introduction of bulbous columns (symbolizing human figures) in the living room and dining room, and the installation of a number of thermals, the half-moon-shaped windows often employed in Ancient Roman and Renaissance architecture. Equally evocative of Classical architecture is the application of faux stone-block wall-paneling in the breakfast room and the stairwells and, in the breakfast room and the hallways, the painting and scoring of the original concrete floors to resemble marble and stone.

Graves's admiration for the work of the English Neoclassical architect Sir John Soane is also apparent in the rotunda, a circular lobby entered through a square-columned portico, and top-lit by a balustraded

Left Neoclassical furnishings and artifacts in the dining room include a set of 19th-century Biedermeier chairs placed around a 19th-century American Federal ebonized wood dining table. The table setting consists of crockery, cutlery, and glassware designed by Michael Graves, and a pair of early 19th-century copies of a Roman bronze candelabra from the 1st century A.D.

Below In the Warehouse's bathroom, a Greco-Roman-style forged-iron, X-frame stool stands next to a sink that is supported on a Classical-style columnar plinth.

oculus (circular opening) set in a domed gallery on the second floor above. Reference to Soane is also evident in the library—a tall, narrow room lined with architectural-style, colonnaded bookcases, and skillfully illuminated with natural light. The height of the library is echoed in the breakfast room and, when contrasted with the lower, compartmentalized ceilings in the living room, dining room, master bedroom, and study, demonstrates how Graves has sensitively manipulated the ceiling heights throughout the house to create varying levels of intimacy or expansiveness according to the primary purpose of each of the individual rooms.

As for the color scheme, it is, apart from the Pompeiian-red fireplace wall in the living room, painted in four shades of white. This recalls the essential elegance and coolness of many 18th-century English Classical-style interiors, and also provides the perfect backdrop against which Graves can display his impressive collection of Neoclassical furniture, and artifacts from, or inspired by, Classical antiquity. Of particular note are the pieces of 19th-century northern European Biedermeier furniture. While drawing heavily on French Empire and English Regency styles of furniture, these pieces also preempt the clean lines and "fitness for purpose" that, one hundred years later, not only came to underpin 20th-century Modernist designs, but also remain clearly evident in Michael Graves's remodeling of the Warehouse and in his dynamic, Postmodernist brand of Classicism.

Left Michael Graves retained the original concrete floor in this hallway, but painted and scored it to resemble Classical-style stone flooring.

Right Reference to Classical architecture in the library is supplied by colonnaded bookcases made from woodgrained plastic. The gilt-rimmed *tondino* (round dish) on the end wall is Italian.

Below A Biedermeier commode furnishes the far end of the hallway shown *left* and supports a Classical-style bronze bust and a pair of bronze *tazzas* (dishes). Neoclassical artifacts in the bedroom beyond include an Empire-style X-frame stool and a circular stone bas relief.

PARIS APARTMENT

"As far as the Directoire style is concerned, Frédéric Méchiche...has long admired its sober, severe lines, and he finds the architecture and furnishings of the final years of the 18th century very contemporary in tone, marrying perfectly with modern art and interiors."

BARBARA STOELTIE

When the prestigious French decorator, Frédéric Méchiche, bought his Parisian residence in the center of the French capital, it consisted of three nondescript apartments on two floors of an old building that had been given a glass-and-aluminum face-lift in the 1960s. The transformation into what, internally, has the appearance of a two-story Directoire-style townhouse is attributable to Méchiche's enthusiasm for late 18th-century French Neoclassicism and to his eye for authentic period detail. However, the "house" also accommodates fixtures, furnishings, and artifacts derived not only from other

Above Frédéric Méchiche's Directoire-style interior also incorporates pieces of art and furniture, such as this 1940s' chair by René Prou, sympathetically chosen from other periods and styles.

Left The Napoleon III chair and stool in the library are uphoistered in a striped fabric–a fashionable pattern in late 18th- and early 19th-century French Neoclassical interiors.

Classical styles and periods, but also from the vocabularies of art and ornament that are as diverse as Ancient Egyptian, Persian, native African, and 20th-century Surrealism.

The successful integration of what, in many instances are heavily contrasting styles of design into a Directoire setting can be largely explained by the essential characteristics of the Directoire style itself. Fashionable in France from the end of Louis XVI's reign (1795), peaking during the rule of the Directoire (1795–99), and enduring until the burgeoning of Empire style in the early 19th century, Directoire

style is a pared-down, sparsely ornamented and rather sober form of Neoclassical decoration that has a very contemporary feel. This is clearly evident in the painted wall-paneling and in the oak parquet, stone-and-marble and limed-board floors. All salvaged from late 18th-century Parisian houses, these, together with other prominent architectural fixtures and fittings, such as a Louis XVI-style wood-and-iron staircase and Directoire-style windows, display a clarity of line that provides an uncluttered and complementary backdrop

Above Neoclassical elements in the hallway include a geometric-pattern tiled floor, a late 18th-century French mahogany chair, and a pair of early 19th-century faux porphyry (variegated stone) urns.

Right Surrounded by early 19th-century Empire-style chairs, two tables with X-frame and tripod bases recall Ancient Greco-Roman-style furniture. The rock crystal chandelier dates from the 18th century.

Above An Ancient Greek marble sculpture stands on a truncated fluted column in the far corner of the living room. Both the Neoclassical Italian chair with buttoned seat-pad and the stripe-upholstered Directoire daybed are late 18th century.

Left Frédéric Méchiche's bedroom features an 18th-century oak parquet floor salvaged from another Parisian apartment and, standing on a whitewashed column, a 19th-century plaster mold of an Ancient Greek vase.

Right Among many Classical artifacts around the apartment is a Roman sculpted stone head dated to 1st century B.C. and a rock crystal obelisk mounted on a Neoclassical bronze base.

for the stylistically eclectic groupings of furniture, artifacts, and fine art that Frédéric Méchiche has thoughtfully arranged throughout the rooms.

Notable among the many pieces of Neoclassical furniture are an early 19th-century stripe-upholstered bench, seat, and matching chairs (signed Janselme); a striped, linen-covered Napoleon III daybed; an early 19th-century cream-and-gilt Italian sofa; a Charles X mahogany games table; and a set of four painted Empire chairs from the Palais de Trianon at Versailles (signed Jacob Desmalter). Happily juxtaposed with these are a number of 20th-century pieces, such as a stripe-upholstered iron seat from the 1940s, a Greco-Roman-style X-frame stool, and a set of wire-back chairs designed by René Prou.

The eclectic composition of furniture is also readily apparent in decorative artifacts that range from an Ancient Greek marble sculpture and a 1st century B.C. Roman head, through a 13th-century Persian bowl and Egyptian and native African masks, to late 20th-century sculptures by César Baldaccini, Eric Schmidt, and Jean Dubuffet. Similarly, Méchiche's collection of fine art encompasses Flemish paintings on wood from the 16th century and, from the 20th century, lithographs and oils by Francis Bacon, an oil by Soulages, drawings by Bérard, sketches by Cocteau and book covers by Picasso and Matisse. Although stylistically diverse, they, like the furnishings, are unified by their design compatibility—a *rapprochement* that lies at the heart of this decorative tour de force.

NEW YORK APARTMENT

"I like a million different things. I like everything. I like every period. I love modern things, and I love 16th-century things. I love antiquities, and I love Louis XVI. I love Art Deco." "For me, the experiences of life, of going to exotic places, of seeing other people's environments, have had a lot of impact."

STEPHEN SILLS

When the influential American decorators Stephen Sills and James Huniford bought their small, 15th-story penthouse on Park Avenue, New York, it was little more than a dilapidated hut on a roof. However, it provided the perfect location for a domestic retreat when working in the city, away from their 12-acre spread in Bedford, New York State. Transformation outside took the form of a large garden terrace. Designed by Huniford, this served as insulation against the frenetic pace of the city streets, and thus reinforced the sense of escape to another time and another place that Sills had conceived for the inside.

Above In the bedroom, a marble column lamp and a collection of fossils and marble artifacts are displayed on an 18th-century Italian inlaid marble table.

Left In the living room, a pair of early 19th-century French globes and a collection of modern geometric sculptures stand on a pair of painted and gilded, marble-top French cabinets. The latter, also early 19th century, are decorated with gilt rosettes.

Much of the inspiration for the interior design and decoration can be traced to Sills's extensive travels overseas, which generated enthusiasm for diverse periods and styles, notably India under the Raj; the Renaissance architecture of Tuscany, Italy; the Art Deco movement and Paris in the 1930s; and the late 18th-century French Neoclassicism under Louis XVI and the Directoire. Once the apartment had been gutted, these influences were brought into play as Sills and Huniford set about "layering the rooms with ornament, pattern, and texture to evoke a kind of visual sedimentation" of all of them.

Above The main feature in the bedroom is a Louis XVI gilded four-poster bed. The obelisk on the trestle table through the doorway provides further reference to late 18th- and early 19th-century Neoclassicism.

Right Artifacts such as a marble bowl and a bronze bust displayed on a marble column, a limestone console table, and a fragment of a carved sandstone tablet recall the archaeological Classicism of the second half of the 18th century.

Thus the backdrop was provided by walls lined with canvas, lightly stenciled with symmetrical, stylized floral repeats framed by architectural moldings, and capped with a "Classical Hellenistic" cast-plaster cornice. Further references to Neoclassical ornamentation were introduced in the form of a Louis XVI limestone fireplace, while Neoclassical furnishings included a Louis XVI gilt four-poster bed; a French Directoire daybed; a Louis XVI-style armchair by Jean-Michel Frank; a pair of early 19th-century French cabinets; and a George III watercolor stand.

Seamlessly positioned among these Neoclassical furnishings were numerous and diverse pieces from other historically significant decorative styles and vocabularies of ornament. Notable examples ranged

Left The frieze and jambs of this Louis XVI limestone fireplace display fluted decoration typical of the simpler and more restrained style of Neoclassical ornamentation fashionable in the late 18th century. In contrast, the pair of gilt firedogs in the hearth, which were made for the Palace of Versailles and fashioned in the form of scrolling acanthus leaves, recalls the more elaborate and flamboyant Classicism of the early 18th century.

Above Sills's and Huniford's skills in the art of "placement" are clearly evident in this display of decorative artifacts. A decorative convention often employed in late 18th- and 19th-century Neoclassical interiors, placement relies for effect on grouping together sometimes seemingly unrelated objects, which in fact have a unity of shape, or texture, or color, or ornament. Here the basic geometric forms inherent in all of the objects brings cohesion to the display.

from a 17th-century Karabach carpet, a Gothic-style screen, and Indian inlaid chairs to a Wiener Werkstätte brass lantern, lamps, and other chairs by Jean-Michel Frank, and contemporary scrubbed oak cabinets designed to conceal a TV, stereo, and books.

All of these items command individual attention, as do the many collections of decorative artifacts on display throughout the apartment. It is, however, their overall esthetic compatibility, and the accompanying sense of historical continuity, that are the most compelling aspects of Sills's and Huniford's design.

GLOSSARY

A

abacus The flat upper part of a *capital supporting an *entablature (*see* Orders). Sometimes plain and sometimes embellished with motifs.

acanthus Foliage ornament based on the serrated leaves of the *Acanthus spinosus* plant, native to the Mediterranean. Similar to thistle, parsley, or poppy leaves and sometimes used for *scrolling foliage.

aegricane Head or skull of a ram or goat, sometimes incorporated in *swags or *festoons. Originated in Ancient Greek and Roman ornament.

anthemion A floral motif similar to the *palmette and based on either the flower of the *acanthus, or the flower and leaf of the honeysuckle.

architrave Collective term for the *moldings surrounding a window, door, panel, or niche.

ashlar Square blocks of stone masonry. Also known as *rusticated masonry.

B

Bacchus Roman god of wine and fertility.

balusters Small posts used in rows to support a handrail. Together they form a balustrade (as on the side of a staircase or a terrace).

baseboard *See* *skirting.

bas-relief A form of sculpture in which the figures or images are slightly raised from the background material (usually stone or plaster) from which they are sculpted.

bead molding A molding consisting of rows of small, convex or semicircular (beadlike) shapes.

bead-and-reel molding Also known as an astragal molding, and consisting of small beadlike shapes (*see* above) alternating with cylindrical shapes inserted at right-angles to them.

brasserie A small table, usually with a circular top on a tripod (three-legged) support, traditionally made of iron or bronze.

bucrania Skulls of sacrificial oxen or bulls, hung with garlands and, like *aegricanes*, sometimes incorporated in *swags or *festoons. Originated in Ancient Greek and Roman ornament.

C

campaign fringing A decorative trim applied to the edges of drapes and upholstery, made of rows of bell-shaped tassels. From the Italian for bell: *campana*.

cantilever A method of supporting any horizontal projection, such as a step(s), balcony, beam, or canopy, with a downward force at only one end— usually through the wall into which one end is keyed. Because no external bracing is used, the projection appears to be self-supporting.

capital The top or head of a column or *pilaster (*see* *Orders).

cartouche A decorative panel consisting of a round, oval, or scroll-shaped frame with either a plain or decorated center.

caryatid A column carved or molded in the form of a draped female figure.

casement A window frame hinged on one side so that it swings out or in to open.

cassoni A richly ornamented marriage chest, with a hinged (often domed) lid.

caulicoli The *fluted stalks of *acanthus leaves, used to support the *volutes on Corinthian *capitals (*see* *Orders).

Ceres Roman goddess of agriculture.

cheval A large glass or mirror hung in a frame and designed to swivel in it.

chimney breast Part of a wall that projects into a room and contains the fireplace and chimney.

chinoiserie Western adaptations of Chinese furnishings, artifacts, and styles of ornament.

closed-string A staircase in which the sides of the treads and risers (the steps) are covered by a sloping member (a string) which supports the *balusters.

Coade stone An artificial cast stone made in London from the 1770s onward, and used for masonry and statuary.

coffered ceiling A ceiling that has been divided into compartments (coffers) by exposed beams or by plaster moldings.

colonnade A row of columns supporting a row of arches or an *entablature.

compartmented Alternative term for *coffered.

consoles Ornamental brackets in the form of scrolls or *volutes. Also a type of table placed against a wall and supported either by consoles, or by between one and four legs.

corbels Stone or timber blocks projecting from the top of a wall and used to support a beam or part of the ceiling above. They are often embellished with decorative carving.

cornice A plain or decorative molding used to cover the join between the walls and the ceiling.

cornucopia A goat's horn overflowing with ears of wheat and various fruits. A symbol of fertility and abundance, and often used as an attribute of *Ceres or *Bacchus.

curricle chair A side-chair.

cyphers Interwoven initials used to form a flat, linear design. Often used as a symbol of patronage or ownership.

D

dado Lower section of a wall, running from floor to approximately waist height, the latter often defined by a wooden or plaster linear molding (a dado rail).

dentil molding A decorative molding made up of regularly spaced "toothlike" blocks. Originally applied as a cornice, but from the 17th century also applied to furniture.

diaper patterns Collective term for patterns incorporating a geometric framework (such as latticework or trelliswork) which is often embellished with decorative motifs and imagery.

Dionysus The Greek equivalent to *Bacchus, Roman god of wine and fertility.

diphrros okladias A cross-legged, Ancient Greek stool with carved animal feet.

Directoire The period following the death of Louis XVI when France was under the rule of the **Directoire** (1795–99). Also used to describe the severe, pared-down style of Neoclassicism that was fashionable in France during that period (*see* Paris Apartment, pages 158–63).

dogleg A staircase with two flights of stairs, in which the upper flight runs parallel to the lower flight and is connected to it by a half-landing.

door frame The framework that surrounds and supports a door. Called doorcase in England.

Doric One of the Classical *Orders.

double-return A staircase that goes up in one flight of stairs and returns to the same level in two flights.

double-sweep A staircase consisting of two curved flights of stairs rising to a communal landing or half-landing above.

drab A brownish-grayish-green paint color that was particularly popular during the first half of the 18th century.

E

eau de nil A pale green color resembling the color of the waters of the River Nile, in Egypt. Also known as Nile green.

egg-and-dart A decorative moulding made up of alternating oval and arrow (or V) shapes.

entablature In Classical architecture, the top of an *Order, made up of an *architrave, a *frieze, and a *cornice.

Etruscan style A style of interior decoration, furniture, ceramics, and other artifacts inspired by the arts and crafts of the ancient civilization of Etruria, centered in Tuscany and part of Umbria in Italy, from the 7th to the 2nd century B.C. Characterized by red, black, and white color schemes, and by motifs such as lions, birds, sphinxes, harpies, and griffins.

F

faux marble Translates from the French as fake marble. A technique for simulating the appearance of marble using paints and glazes.

festoon In Classical Roman ornament a fruit and floral garland, often also containing *aegricanes and *bucrania, hung from the *friezes of temples. During the Renaissance and thereafter often included *rosettes, lion masks, and *putti in place of the *aegricanes* and *bucrania*.

field The section of a wall that extends down from the *cornice or *frieze to the top of the *dado.

fielded Raised, as in the raised center panels of doors and wall-paneling.

finial A carved, cast, or molded ornament on top of a spire, gable, or post. Also used on the ends of curtain rods. Typical forms include acorns, arrow heads, and pinecones.

flambeaux A flaming torch. A symbol of life in Ancient Greece, and an attribute of Venus, Roman goddess of love.

floorcloth A floor-covering made from canvas stiffened with linseed oil, and then either painted or stenciled with patterns (often to resemble more expensive coverings such as *parquet, marble, granite, and even carpet).

flying stairs A staircase in which the flight or flights of stairs are *cantilevered from the wall(s) of the stairwell, and have no *newel.

frieze The section of wall extending from the ceiling or *cornice down to the top of the *field. Usually embellished with decorative motifs.

G

gable The part of a wall directly underneath the end of a pitched roof, cut into a triangular shape by the sloping sides of the roof.

girandole A convex mirror.

Greco-Roman Collective term for the Classical architecture, ornament, and decoration of Ancient Greece and Rome.

Greek key A pattern made up of regularly repeated, interlocking right-angled and vertical lines. Used as a border ornament.

greenery-yallery A yellowish-olive green color, especially popular during the second half of the 19th century.

grisaille A monochromatic *trompe l'oeil technique in which figures and patterns are rendered in shades of black, gray, and white.

grotesques Decorations based on Ancient Roman wall paintings. Typical motifs included animals, birds, and fishes.

guilloche A form of decoration or ornament made up of interlacing curved bands, sometimes forming circles embellished with floral motifs.

H

herms A rectangular pillar or post, tapering toward the base and terminating at the top in a head or a bust (often of Hermes, the Greek messenger of the gods).

I, J

Ionic One of the Classical *Orders.

jambs The straight, vertical sides of a doorway, an arch, or a fireplace–in the case of the latter, flanking the hearth and sometimes in the form of *pilasters.

K

key stone The central stone in the curve of an arch.

kline A type of bench used in Ancient Greece for reclining while eating, as well as sleeping.

klismos A type of Ancient Greek chair, armless, with inwardly curving legs and a horizontal, curved back-support. Variations on this basic design were also produced by the Romans.

L

lintel A supporting beam across the top of an opening, such as a doorway, a window, or a hearth.

lit à la duchesse A type of bed, of French origin, with head-posts that support a canopy that extends halfway down the length of the bed.

lit à la polonaise A type of bed with a domed canopy secured by fabric-covered rods curving up to it from posts at the four corners of the bed. Named after the French king, Louis XV's Polish wife.

lit d'ange A type of post-less bed, of French origin, with a "flying" canopy secured to the wall behind and extending over part of the length of the bed.

lit-en-bateau French term for a bed with outwardly curving head- and foot-boards (of equal height), their shape approximating to the bow and stern of a *bateau* (a boat).

M

marquetry A form of inlay work, mostly used on furniture, in which pieces of different colored woods, ivory, or metal are set into a surface to form decorative patterns.

medallions Circular or oval decorative devices, usually bearing a portrait or other imagery, and applied to plasterwork, silver, porcelain, and textiles.

mensa lunata A *console table with a semicircular top, the straight back of which is placed against a wall.

moldings See pages 52–55.

mullions Upright vertical bars used to vertically divide windows and other openings. Also fixed or hinged, vertically divided windows.

N

newel The post at the end of a staircase, usually attached to the handrail and the string (see open-string). On circular or winding staircases the newel is also the central post around which the stairs curve, and which supports the narrow side of the steps.

O

oculus A circular opening (sometimes glazed) in a wall or floor, or in the top of a dome.

open-string A staircase in which the side or sides of the treads and risers (the steps) are not enclosed by a string (see *closed-string), and are therefore visible.

Orders The architectural components that constitute the basis of Classical Greek and Roman architecture. Each Order consists of a *column, usually rising from a *pedestal or *plinth, topped by a *capital and an *abacus, and supporting an *entablature. The various styles of Order include: Doric, Ionic, Corinthian, Composite, and Tuscan (see pages 10–11).

ormolu An alloy of copper, zinc, and sometimes tin. Also gold leaf when prepared for gilding bronze.

P

overmantel The decorative treatment of the area of wall above a fireplace, often incorporating a framed painting or mirror.

palmette A foliate motif, loosely based on a stylized palm leaf and often indistinguishable from an *anthemion.

Parian ware Artifacts, especially busts, made from a type of porcelain with a semi-matte finish. Originally called statuary porcelain, and known as Parian because of its resemblance to the white marble found on the Greek island of Paros.

parquetry Thin strips of different colored hardwoods laid over a subfloor to form a pattern.

passementier A person skilled in the art of making decorative trimmings, such as tassels, braids, and fringes (*see* *campaign fringing), for soft furnishings.

pateras Oval- or circular-shaped motifs based on dishes used in religious ceremonies. Usually decorated with a central stylized flower and/or *fluting. They are sometimes indistinguishable from *rosettes.

pedestal The supporting base for a column or an artifact such as a statue or a vase.

pediment A low-pitched (triangular-shaped) *gable across the top of a *portico, door, window, or fireplace. When the top of the triangular shape is omitted or left open, it is called a broken pediment.

Pegasus The winged horse of Classical mythology.

pier glass A tall, narrow, often ornately framed mirror traditionally hung between two windows.

pilaster A flat, rectangular Classical column fixed to a wall. Often used to frame a doorway, or the doors of a piece of furniture, or as the *jambs of a fireplace.

plinth The square block below the base of a column or *pilaster.

Pompeiian Style of architecture, ornament, and decoration found in, and inspired by, the Ancient Roman town of Pompeii, rediscovered in southern Italy during the mid-18th century.

porphyry A hard, fine-grained rock, usually dark red or purple, but sometimes gray or green, and flecked with white crystals.

portico A roofed entrance porch, usually supported by columns.

Postmodernism An architectural and design movement that began in the mid-1970s as a reaction to the plain, unadorned forms of Modernism, and which revived many of the Classical forms of architecture and ornament.

print room A decorative convention that emerged in the mid-18th century, which involved decorating a room with prints or engravings pasted on to the walls (and sometimes doors).

putti Type of ornament depicting small, chubby infants—usually represented as the attendants of Eros and Cupid, the Greek and Roman gods of love.

R

récamier French term for a couch or settee, used for both sitting and lying on.

reeded A surface decorated with parallel strips of narrow convex moldings divided by grooves.

rectilinear In a straight line, or lines, and bounded by straight lines.

rocaille A form of ornament prevalent in Rococo style. Based on asymmetrical rock and shell forms.

rosettes Circular, formalized floral ornament. Also *see* *pateras.

rosso antico A type of marble with predominantly red and yellow colored veins.

rusticated masonry Alternative name for *ashlar.

S

scagliola A type of multicolored plaster or *stucco which, when polished, resembles marble.

scrolling foliage A pattern or form of ornament consisting of scrolling, curving, or trailing plant forms, such as grapevines or *acanthus plants.

serliana Alternative name for a *Venetian window.

singeries French for monkeys, and a style of pictorial decoration, popular in Rococo interiors, depicting monkeys engaged in human activities (often set within *scrolling foliage).

skirting The wooden board placed around the base of an internal wall at the junction of the floor and the wall; often molded or grooved along the top.

slips The fascia often installed between the opening of a hearth and the *jambs and the *frieze or *lintel of a mantelpiece.

spandrels The approximately triangular-shaped spaces between an arched opening and the rectangle formed by any linear *moldings surrounding it. These spaces are often decorated with motifs.

spiral staircase A type of staircase in which the flight of stairs winds around a central column or *newel, the narrow ends of the stairs being supported by the newel. Also known as a newel, or *winding stair.

straight flight A type of staircase which connects floors by a single, straight flight of stairs.

strapwork Form of ornament consisting of twisted and interlaced bands (similar in appearance to strips of leather or ribbons). Sometimes combined with *grotesques, and often studded with *rosettes, or faceted, jewellike forms–the latter known as jeweled strapwork.

stucco A fine cement or plaster applied to the surface of walls and *moldings.

swags Loops of drapery; also pendant garlands of flowers, fruits, vegetables, leaves, or shells.

T

tazzas Wine cups with a shallow, circular bowl.

thermals Semicircular windows subdivided into three sections by two *mullions. Also known as Diocletian windows from their use in the *thermae* (the public baths) of the Roman Emperor Diocletian.

thronos A type of Ancient Greek chair, with carved rams' heads at the arm-ends, and a back often shaped like a snake or a horse's head.

tondino An Italian term for a round dish with a broad, flat rim and a sunken center.

transom The horizontal component running across the top or middle of doors or windows.

trompe l'oeil French for "trick of the eye." A decorative technique in which paints or dyes are applied to a flat surface to create the appearance of three-dimensional scenes or objects.

tympanum The area between the *lintel of a doorway and the arch above it. Also the triangular space enclosed by the moldings of a pediment.

V

vaulted Arched, as in an arch-shaped roof or ceiling.

Venetian window A window with an arch-top center section flanked by two narrower rectangular sections. Also known as a *serliana*.

volute A spiral, scrolling form, probably based on the shape of a ram's horn.

W

wall-strings Diagonal or inclined timbers attached to the wall of a stairwell, into which one or both sides of the steps of a staircase are secured.

wave-scroll An undulating, linear, wavelike pattern based on a series of scrolling C or S shapes. Sometimes elaborated into *scrolling foliage.

winding stairs *See* *spiral staircase.

wrought iron Iron that has been beaten or bent into shape, as opposed to being cast in a mold.

DIRECTORY

Bernd Goeckler
Bernd Goeckler Antiques, Inc.
30 East 10th Street
New York
New York 10003
U.S.A.
Antique dealer

Borja Azcarate
"Gustavianaæ"
c/Lagasca 38
28001
Madrid
Spain
Interior designer

Brian Juhos
Flat 119
25 Porchester Place
London W2 2PF
England
Interior designer

Brunschwig & Fils
10 The Chambers
Chelsea Harbour Design Centre
London SW10 OXF
England
Also at:
979 Third Avenue
New York
New York 10022–1234
U.S.A.
Period fabrics

Chartered Society of Designers
29 Bedford Square
London WC1B 3EG
England

Crown Berger Ltd
Crown House
P.O. Box 37
Holins Road
Darwen, Lancashire BB3 OBG
England
Paints

Crowther of Syon Lodge
Busch Corner
London Road
Isleworth
Middlesex TW7 5BH
England
Architectural components and statuary

Frédéric Méchiche
4 rue de Thorigny
75003
Paris
France
Interior designer

H. & R. Johnson
Highgate Tile Works
High Street, Turnstall
Stoke-on-Trent
Staffordshire ST6 4JX
England
Also at:
Johnson USA Inc.
P.O. Box 2325
Farmingdale
New Jersey 07727
U.S.A.
Ceramic tiles

Joinery Spec Ltd
Unit 2, St Clements Centre
St Clements Road, Nechells
Birmingham B7 5AF
Staircases, paneling, and windows

Junkers
Wheaton Court
Commercial Centre
Wheaton Road
Witham, Essex CM8 3UJ
England
Also at:
4920 East Landon Drive
Anaheim
California 92807
U.S.A.
Wooden flooring

Lelièvre
101 Cleveland Street
London W1P 5PN
England
Fabrics

Manolo Morales
Trajano 52
41002
Seville
Spain
Interior designer

Materials Unlimited
2 West Michigan Avenue
Ypsilanti
Michigan 48197
U.S.A.
New and reclaimed architectural materials and antique furniture

Michael Graves, Architect
341 Nassau Street
Princeton
New Jersey 08540
U.S.A.
Also at:
560 Broadway
Suite 401
New York
New York 10012
U.S.A.
Architect and designer

O'Shea Galleries
120A Mount Street
London W1Y 5HB
England
Archive pictures

Stephen Sills & James Huniford
Stephen Sills Associates
30 East 67th Street
New York
New York 10021
U.S.A.
Interior designers and decorators

The American Society of Interior Designers
608 Massachusetts Avenue NE
Washington, D.C. 20002
U.S.A.

UK Marble Ltd
21 Nurcott Road
Hereford HR4 9LW
England
Marble and granite flooring, paneling, fireplaces, and architectural moldings

Yves Gastou
Galerie Yves Gastou
12 Rue Bonaparte
Paris 6e
France
Interior designer

Zoffany
Talbot House
17 Church Street
Rickmansworth
Hertfordshire
WD3 1DE
England
Also at:
Whittaker & Woods
5100 Highlands Parkway
Smyrna
Georgia 30082
U.S.A.
Fabrics and wallpapers

Zuber & Cie
42 Pimlico Road
London SW1W 8LP
England
Also at:
D & D Building
979 Third Avenue
New York
New York 10022
U.S.A.
Fabrics and wallpapers

INDEX

ACKNOWLEDGMENTS

I would like to thank Tim Clinch for his wonderful photography, and for his enthusiasm and commitment to the book. I would also like to thank the team at Mitchell Beazley for their skills and dedication: Janis Utton and Tony Spalding for design and layout; Judith More for overseeing the project; Julia North for running it; Claire Weatherall for contributing; Hilary Bird for the index; Jane Royston for proofreading; Paul Hammond for production control; Amanda Jones for US rights; and Arlene Sobel for her editing and her unflagging patience, encouragement, and good humor. I would also like to offer heartfelt thanks to the following for allowing us to photograph their homes and/or their work: Borja Azcarate; Bill Blass; Victor Cornelius; Yves Gastou; Bernd Goeckler; Michael Graves; Fayal Greene; Monsieur and Madame Holder; Peter Hone; Richard Jenrette; Brian Juhos; Frédéric Méchiche; Manolo Morales; Stephen Sills and James Huniford; Joan Thring; David Whitcomb; and Lillian Williams.

Picture Credits

AKG, London (41 l)/Erich Lessing (11 br, 13 br).
Arcaid/Richard Bryant (14, 25 br (by kind permission of 'The Mount Vernon Ladies Association of the Union'), 30, 31 bl, 31 br)/Niall Clutton (39 tl)/Mark Fiennes (31 tl).
Archive pictures supplied by courtesy of Raymond O'Shea, the O'Shea Galleries, London (3, 5, 7, 10, 12, 28, 176).
Bridgeman Art Library/John Bethell (39 r)/Central Saint Martins College of Art and Design (18)/Museo Archeologico Nazionale, Naples (11 tl).
Tim Clinch/Interior Archive (48, 53, 57, 69, 80, 90, 96, 122, 124, 129).

Corbis UK Ltd/Adam Woolfitt (11 bl, 13 tl).
English Heritage (16, 17 bl, 22, 38 tl, 39 bl).
E.T. Archive (13 bl, 13 tr, 17 tl, 20 t, 20–21 b, 21 br, 25 bl).
Robert Harding Picture Library/N. Francis (43 r).
John Heseltine (38 r, 40 bl).
The Interior Archive/Laura Rosen (40 tl)/Fritz von der Schulenberg (19 tl, 31 tr, 32, 41 r).
National Trust Photographic Library/Bill Batten (19 bl)/John Bethell (19 tr).
Reed Consumer Books Limited/Tommy Candler (author's picture)/Tim Clinch (front jacket, back jacket, endpapers, 1, 2–3, 4–5, 6, 8, 11 tr, 21 t, 29 br, 34, 35 tr, 40 r, 43 tl, 43 bl, 44 l, 45 r, 45 l, 49, 52, 54, 56,

58, 60, 61, 62, 64, 65, 67, 70, 73, 76, 77, 78, 79, 81, 82, 83, 84, 85, 86, 87, 88, 89, 90, 91, 92, 94, 95, 97, 98, 99, 100, 102, 103, 104, 105, 106, 108, 109, 110, 111, 112, 113, 114, 115, 116, 117, 118, 121, 123, 125, 126, 128, 129, 130, 132, 134, 135, 136, 137, 138, 140, 141, 142, 143, 144, 145, 146, 147, 148, 149, 150, 151, 152, 154, 155, 156, 157, 158, 159, 160, 162, 163)/Tim Ridley/ Greenwich Hospital (29 tl)/James Merrell (17 br, Owner Lillian Williams, 17 tr, 24, 25 t, 26, 29 tr, 35 tl, 41 tr, 42 r, 44 r, 46, 50, 55, 66, 68, 70, 71, 72, 74, 75, 97, 120, 127, 164, 165, 166, 168, 169)/Kim Sayer (19 b, 29 bl, 35 b, 36, 38 bl, 42 l, 51, 59).
Fabrics for endpapers by Lelièvre.